If *These* WALLS *Could* TALK:
MONTREAL CANADIENS

If These **WALLS** Could **TALK:**

MONTREAL CANADIENS:

Stories from the
Montreal Canadiens Ice,
Locker Room, and Press Box

Pat Hickey

TRIUMPH
BOOKS

Library of Congress Cataloging-in-Publication Data

Names: Hickey, Pat, 1944- author.

Title: If these walls could talk : Montreal Canadiens : stories from the Montreal Canadiens' ice, locker room, and press box / Pat Hickey.

Description: Chicago, Illinois : Triumph Books LLC, [2018]

Identifiers: LCCN 2018023915 | ISBN 9781629375205

Subjects: LCSH: Montreal Canadiens (Hockey team)—Anecdotes. | Hockey—Canada—Anecdotes. | Montreal Canadiens (Hockey team)— History. | Hockey—Canada—History.

Classification: LCC GV848.M6 H55 2018 | DDC 796.962/6409714254—dc23

LC record available at https://lccn.loc.gov/2018023915

This book is available in quantity at special discounts for your group or organization. For further information, contact:

Triumph Books LLC
814 North Franklin Street
Chicago, Illinois 60610
(312) 939-3330
www.triumphbooks.com

Printed in U.S.A.

ISBN: 978-1-62937-520-5

Design by Amy Carter

For Red Fisher, 1926–2018,
colleague, mentor, friend,
R. I. P.

CONTENTS

CHAPTER 1
THE GOOD OL' DAYS

When a player joins the Canadiens for the first time, he talks about how proud he is to be part of the most successful franchise in NHL history. He might have grown up cheering for the Maple Leafs, the Rangers, or the Oilers, but he talks about the thrill of putting on the iconic sweater with the CH logo for the first time.

You overlook the fact the kid probably wasn't born when the Canadiens won the last of their record 24 Stanley Cups.

The Canadiens haven't won the Stanley Cup since 1993. This is a long-standing cause for concern among the team's large and devoted fan base, particularly the partisans of a certain age who remember when Lord Stanley's gift to hockey took up semi-permanent residence in Montreal.

The Canadiens won the Cup fives times in the 1950s, five times in the 1960s, and six times in the 1970s. When legendary Mayor Jean Drapeau announced that "the parade would follow the usual route," nobody had to be reminded that a cavalcade of convertibles would transport the players and the Cup from City Hall and head west on Ste. Catherine Street before finally arriving at the Montreal Forum.

Those decades were filled with magic names——Richard, Béliveau, Lafleur, Robinson, Savard, Plante, Dryden. Twenty-seven players from those three eras would be elected to the Hockey Hall of Fame, and you can also find coaches Toe Blake and Scotty Bowman enshrined there along with general managers Frank Selke and Sam Pollock and owner Hartland Molson.

Those were simpler times, and everything fell into place for the Canadiens in that golden era.

For starters, the odds of winning the Cup were better because there were fewer teams competing for the Cup.

Seven of those Cups were won when the NHL consisted of six teams, and there were only two rounds of playoffs. There were never more than 18 teams in the Bowman era of the 1970s, and a successful playoff run meant winning 12 games, four fewer than today.

There was no amateur draft when the Canadiens began their run. Teams were assigned territorial rights, and they developed players through junior and amateur senior teams, which they owned. Montreal had access to most of the top youngsters in Quebec and also developed players on junior teams in Peterborough, Ontario, and Regina.

Jean Béliveau played for the Quebec Aces, a team in the Quebec Senior League. The Canadiens owned his professional rights but Béliveau was happy to remain in Quebec. The Aces were nominally an amateur team although he was well compensated for his efforts. The Canadiens solved the problem by buying the entire league and changing its designation to that of a professional league.

There was no salary cap in those days, but the players didn't make a lot of money either.

"You had to find something to do to tide you over in the summer," recalled Hall of Famer Dickie Moore, who owned a Dairy Queen franchise before launching a million-dollar business renting tools, heavy equipment, and construction trailers.

Bobby Rousseau was a golf professional, and it wasn't unusual to find your favorite player working on the back of a Molson beer truck.

3

Maurice (Rocket) Richard made $50,000 in his best season. That was good money in the 1950s, but if you combined Richard's total earnings with the Canadiens, it would be less than the current NHL minimum wage of $650,000.

The draft was introduced in 1963, but the effects of the draft didn't catch up to the Canadiens until the 1980s. When the league expanded from six to 12 teams in 1969, Sam Pollock had a stockpile of players under contract, and he sent these players and some aging NHLers to the expansion teams in return for draft picks.

Those deals allowed Montreal to pick Guy Lafleur with the first overall pick in 1971; Steve Shutt at No. 4 in 1972, Bob Gainey with the eighth pick in 1973, and Doug Risebrough at No. 7 in 1974.

The draft has not been as productive for the Canadiens since they selected Doug Wickenheiser with the first overall pick in 1980. In the intervening years, the Canadiens have had only nine top-10 draft picks.

Current general manager Marc Bergevin has stressed the importance of building through the draft, but he has also noted that it isn't easy when 20 or so teams are picking ahead of you.

In 2001, the Canadiens missed the playoffs for the third consecutive year, and my son Simon, who was nine at the time, asked: "How come the Canadiens always suck?"

This chapter is a history lesson for Simon and the generation of Canadiens fans who roll their eyes when their fathers and grandfathers talk about the parade of Hall of Fame players who forged three unforgettable dynasties.

The Flying '50s

Two key personnel changes—one on the ice and one behind the bench—helped produce the team known as the Flying Frenchmen. The key addition on the ice was Jean Béliveau whose résumé would include 10 Stanley Cup victories spread over three decades. Béliveau was reluctantly wrested away from the Quebec Aces senior team in 1953 and joined a high-powered offense that included Maurice (Rocket) Richard, Bernie (Boom Boom) Geoffrion, Dickie Moore, and Henri (Pocket Rocket) Richard.

The change behind the bench involved Hector (Toe) Blake, who had once been the Rocket's linemate. He replaced Dick Irvin in 1955 and promptly led Montreal to the first of five consecutive Stanley Cups. He retired in 1968 after winning a record eighth Cup.

Irvin won his third Stanley Cup with the Canadiens in 1953 and took the team to the final in each of the next two seasons. But General Manager Frank Selke was not a fan of Irvin's coaching philosophy. While the Canadiens had one of the greatest collections of highly skilled players in NHL history, Irvin emphasized toughness that bordered on goonery. Some believed that Irvin's style contributed to one of the major blots on the team's history—the Richard Riot.

On March 13, 1955, Hal Laycoe high-sticked Richard, opening a cut on his face. Richard responded by throwing several haymakers in Laycoe's direction. When linesman Cliff Thompson tried to intervene, Richard punched him.

Richard wasn't a first-time offender, and he had several previous run-ins with NHL president Clarence Campbell. The incident gave Campbell an opportunity to teach Richard a lesson, and he suspended the Canadiens star for the three remaining games in the regular season as well as the entire playoffs.

Montreal fans viewed Campbell's reaction as unfair, and he made what proved to be a bad decision when he attended the Canadiens game against the Detroit Red Wings on March 17. Campbell was pelted with vegetables and punched by a fan. After someone set off a smoke bomb following the first period, the game was forfeited to the Red Wings.

As fans poured out of the Forum, a riot erupted. The crowd surged down Ste. Catherine Street to the downtown core, breaking windows and looting stores. Police officers who tried to quell the disturbance were pelted with rocks and garbage.

In the aftermath of the riot, Selke decided a coaching change was in order. Blake, who had been coaching a variety of Canadiens' farm teams since a broken ankle ended his NHL career in 1948, was summoned to Montreal. While Blake was no shrinking violet when it came to challenging authority, Selke figured that he could serve as a moderating influence on Richard, who had once been described as "two sticks of dynamite searching for a match."

It was the second time Blake had been called on to bolster Richard. In 1943, Irvin put Blake at left wing on a line with Elmer Lach at centre and Richard on the right side. He thought the bilingual Blake would be able to complement the French-speaking Richard and the English-speaking Lach. The result was the Punch Line, which was the dominant line in the late 1940s. In their five seasons together, Lach won two scoring titles and Richard became the first player to score 50 goals in a season.

Even without Richard, the Canadiens had enough talent to reach the final of the Stanley Cup playoffs in 1955, losing to Detroit in a seven-game final. The suspension weighed heavily on Richard as he watched from the sidelines. He felt a responsibility for the loss. He apologized to Montreal fans and said he was determined to win the Cup the following season.

Richard made good on that promise. The Canadiens won the Cup in 1956 to begin a string of five consecutive championship seasons. How dominant were those teams? The Canadiens won 10 playoff series in that run and never went to a seventh game. Only two of the series went to six games and Montreal swept Chicago and Toronto to complete the run in 1960. During the streak, the Canadiens won 40 playoff games and lost only nine.

The Canadiens had so much firepower that the NHL was forced to change its rules regarding power plays. In that era, players were required to serve the full two minutes following a minor penalty, and a team could score more than once on a single power play.

The sentiment to change the rule grew after Béliveau scored three times during a single power play.

It happened on November 5, 1955, and the Canadiens were trailing Boston 2–0 when Cal Gardner was sent off as the first period ended. It became a two-man advantage when Hal Laycoe was penalized 16 seconds into the second period.

The Bruins were faced with the unenviable task of defending against a power-play unit that consisted of five future Hall of Famers. Norris Trophy winners Doug Harvey and Tom Johnson were at the points; Béliveau, Maurice Richard, and Bert Olmstead were up front.

Forty-two seconds into the period, Béliveau took Olmstead's pass from the corner and redirected it behind Bruins goaltender Terry Sawchuk for his first goal of the evening. He converted another pass from Olmstead at 1:06, and Gardner and Laycoe were still in the penalty box when Béliveau completed his hat trick at 1:26 with Olmstead again setting up the play.

Béliveau needed only 44 seconds to string together the fastest hat trick in Canadiens history, with all three markers coming during the same power play. The only NHL player to score three goals in a shorter span was Chicago's Bill Mosienko, who scored three even-strength goals in 21 seconds against the New York Rangers on March 23, 1952.

Béliveau added a fourth goal at even strength to complete Montreal's 4–2 victory.

In Andy O'Brien's book, *Fire-Wagon Hockey*, Béliveau recalled that he was disappointed with his play going into the Boston game. Through the first dozen games, he had scored only three goals.

"I don't think I was ever so discouraged as I was at the start of the 1955–56 season," Béliveau said. "I must have hit fifteen goal posts before Toe Blake told me to start shooting at the net, rather than at a particular spot, until I broke my slump. Sure enough, a couple did, and I did all right."

Béliveau's hat trick wasn't the only time the Canadiens cashed in big on the power play that season. On seven other occasions, the Canadiens scored twice during a single power play.

At the end of the season, the league considered a change that would allow a player to leave the penalty box after a goal was scored. Frank Selke argued that the rule specifically targeted the Canadiens. He noted that there had been no complaints in previous seasons when Detroit and Chicago scored multiple goals during a power play. Selke's plea fell on deaf ears. The new rule was passed after a 5–1 vote with Montreal casting the lone dissenting vote.

The Swinging '60s

Charlie Fleischer, a comedian and actor best known as the voice of Roger Rabbit, is credited with first saying: "If you remember the '60s, you weren't really there."

But the Canadiens created many memorable moments in a decade that was defined by the rivalry between the Canadiens and the Toronto Maple Leafs. The Canadiens won the Stanley Cup five times and the Maple Leafs won it four times.

Toe Blake (in his signature fedora) reaches out to goalie Gump Worsley on the ice as his players celebrate their 3–2 in overtime win over the Detroit Red Wings on May 5, 1966 to clinch the Stanley Cup. *(AP Photo)*

The Canadiens became Béliveau's team in the 1960s. After Rocket Richard retired in 1960, Doug Harvey became captain, but he was traded to the New York Rangers a year later after he became involved in the failed attempt to form a players' union. Béliveau would wear the C until he retired in 1971.

Toe Blake was behind the bench for four of the Cup wins in the 1960s with Claude Ruel guiding the 1969 team.

This was a decade of change. Hall of Famer Bernie (Boom Boom) Geoffrion had his nose out of joint because he wasn't offered the captain's job. He felt he had earned the job because he showed his dedication to the team by battling through numerous injuries. He retired to coach the Quebec Aces but returned to the NHL two years later with the Rangers.

The Canadiens prospered with Béliveau, Henri Richard, Claude Provost, J.C. Tremblay, Jacques Laperriere, tough guy John Ferguson, and the goaltending triumverate of Lorne (Gump) Worsley, Charlie Hodge, and Rogie Vachon. The latter years of the decade provided a glimpse of the future as Hall of Famers Serge Savard and Yvan Cournoyer made their NHL debuts.

Blake, who would retire after winning his record eighth Stanley Cup, drove his players to greatness, but he was occasionally shortsighted when evaluating talent.

For example, he never recognized Red Berenson's potential, dismissing him because he played college hockey at the University of Michigan. Berenson had a similar experience after he was traded to the Rangers but emerged as one of the first stars of the expansion era with the St. Louis Blues. He was part of the Canadian team that beat the Soviet Union in the 1972

Summit Series, and he later turned to coaching, winning the Jack Adams Trophy as the NHL's coach of the year in 1981 with the Blues before beginning a 33-year career as head coach at Michigan.

Blake also underestimated Hall of Famer Yvan Cournoyer.

"He didn't think I could play defense because I was small, and the only time I was on the ice was when we were on the power play," said Cournoyer. In his first four seasons under Blake, he scored 54 goals, and 41 of them were on the power play. "He was a good coach, but I was happy when Piton (Claude Ruel) took over and he let me play."

The transition went beyond the change in personnel. The league underwent a radical transformation in the 1967–68 season when it expanded from six to 12 teams.

Expansion turned Blake's world upside down, and, at 56, he elected to leave on his own terms. He said that he didn't need the pressure that came with the job.

For 13 years as a Hall of Fame player and 13 years as a coach, he had settled into a comfortable routine.

The Original Six teams were close enough that teams traveled by train. Players were often together for their entire careers and formed strong bonds.

"It was easy to motivate us because we hated the guys on the other team," the late Dollard St. Laurent once told me. "We'd play the Blackhawks at home on a Saturday night and then both teams would get on the same train to go to Chicago for a Sunday night game. Our cars were at different ends of the train, and we had staggered hours for breakfast so the teams never met."

11

Blake would kill time on the train by playing gin rummy with the *Montreal Star*'s Red Fisher.

"He was my personal bank," said Fisher, a claim that was routinely dismissed by the competitive Blake. Expansion brought plane rides to Minnesota, Pittsburgh, St. Louis, and California. In the era before charter flights, this meant long, uncomfortable flights on commercial aircraft.

There was also one more round in the playoffs, but that was a mere annoyance for Blake, whose 1968 team went 12–1 in the playoffs. The Canadiens swept St. Louis in the final, but each game was decided by one goal. The coach of the Blues was Scotty Bowman, and the team's leading scorer was Red Berenson.

After he stopped coaching, Blake would remain with the team as a consultant, and he mentored Bowman, who would eclipse Blake's record in 2002, winning his ninth Stanley Cup with the Red Wings.

"I always admired Toe so much," he said in an interview announcing his own retirement after beating the Carolina Hurricanes. "What I might have admired most about him was that he won his last game as coach against us in 1968. I thought, 'What a neat way to go out. Most times coaches lose their last game and get fired. It's not easy to walk away when you win.'"

Blake left behind a great legacy and also set the table for what would be the most successful decade in franchise history.

1970s

The Canadiens ushered in a new decade with a Stanley Cup win in 1971 when goaltender Ken Dryden took time out from his law studies at McGill University to win the Conn Smythe Trophy as the most valuable player in the playoffs. The victory wasn't enough to save head coach Al MacNeil, who was a victim of the growing nationalism in Quebec. Because MacNeil didn't

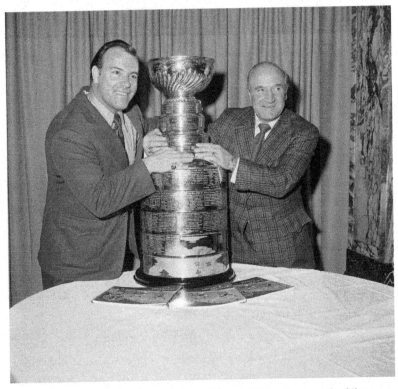

Scotty Bowman (left), coach of the Canadiens, and Billy Reay, coach of the Chicago Blackhawks, pose with a replica before the start of the 1973 Stanley Cup Final. *(AP Photo)*

speak French, he was exiled to the Canadiens' farm team in his native Nova Scotia.

The Canadiens turned to Montreal native Scotty Bowman. His promising career as a player ended in junior hockey when Jean-Guy Talbot was chasing him on a breakaway and swung his stick in frustration. The result was a fractured skull and a five-inch gash in his head. Bowman played junior hockey for another two years, but he experienced numerous headaches and turned to coaching.

He enjoyed success in the Canadiens organization, winning a Memorial Cup with the Hull-Ottawa Junior Canadiens and then moving on to Peterborough.

He signed on as an assistant coach with the expansion team the St. Louis Blues in 1968 and became the head coach when Lynn Patrick stepped down early in the team's inaugural season.

When the NHL added six teams in the first expansion, it created two divisions with the so-called Original Six in one division and the new teams in the other division. That guaranteed an expansion team a place in the Stanley Cup Final, and Bowman guided the Blues to the final in each of their first three seasons. One interesting side note is that Bowman brought in Talbot to provide leadership and stability to the Blue line.

As the Canadiens were parting ways with MacNeil, Bowman was feuding with the Blues' management over his contract, and he welcomed the opportunity to come home.

Bowman built on the Canadiens' winning tradition by guiding the team to five Stanley Cup victories in eight seasons. He established a reputation as a hard-driving taskmaster.

"Scotty was all about challenges," recalled Peter Mahovlich, a free spirit who presented the coach with a challenge or two.

"No matter what you did, how good you were, Scotty would challenge you to be better. We won in 1973, and then Philadelphia won two Stanley Cups and Scotty challenged us to win three. And when we won three, he wanted four and we got it.

"If we had the most goals, he'd challenge us to cut down on our goals-against. One season, we were way ahead of everyone in the standings, and he challenged us to beat Boston's record for the most points in a season. We did that and the next season we did even better."

That was the 1976–77 season when the Canadiens posted the best record in NHL history, amassing 132 points on a 60–8–12 record.

"We lost eight games all season, and Scotty was on us after every one of those losses," said Guy Lafleur. "He didn't think we should ever lose."

"He was not only upset when we lost, but he was also upset when we tied, and he was upset when we won the game but we didn't play up to the way he thought we should play," said Réjean Houle.

Peter Mahovlich was an elite player who was part of Team Canada for the 1972 Summit Series against the Soviet Union. His shorthanded goal in Game 2 was a crucial part of Canada's eventual victory. On five occasions, he scored 34 or more goals for the Canadiens.

But he had a way of frustrating Bowman. He's an outgoing type, the polar opposite of his taciturn brother Frank. Peter Mahovlich liked to have a good time and frequented bars on Montreal's Crescent Street and Station 10, a dive bar within stumbling distance of the Forum, where he recalls drinking with baseball stars Johnny Bench, Pete Rose, and Lou Brock.

Bowman disapproved of Mahovlich's public carousing and exacted a price in practice.

"We would skate hard after practice, and after one or two trips down the ice, Scotty would tell Cournoyer and Henri (Richard) they were finished," said Mahovlich. "We'd go back and forth again and he'd tell a few more guys they could leave. That went on until there were only two guys left—me and Jimmy Roberts. We'd do two more trips and then Scotty would blow his whistle and say we're through.

"That's when I said: 'C'mon Scotty, can't we do more?' Scotty exploded and then he blew his whistle so hard that the pea came out and he's standing there with a whistle that doesn't work. He wasn't taking any chances the next day—he came out with a new whistle and a couple of horns on his wrist."

Mahovlich said Bowman's strength was that he didn't feel he needed to be friends with his players.

"He knew that you can't be friends in this business, you have to treat players as professionals, but you can't allow a friendship to get in the way," said Mahovlich. "That was a change for some guys because (Claude) Ruel wanted to be like one of the boys and Al MacNeil's nature was to be a good guy who liked everyone.

"Five years down the road, you began to appreciate what you accomplished because of Scotty," said Mahovlich. "But it was tough when you were playing for him."

"You didn't appreciate him until you were skating around the ice with the Stanley Cup," said Murray Wilson. "A lot of the guys will tell you that they hated him, hated playing for him, but he made you a better player."

"People look at the talent on those teams—and we had 13 players who are in the Hall of Fame—and they say we should have won with all those stars, but it's not an easy job to handle a team with that much talent," said Réjean Houle. "You're dealing with huge egos and you have to make sure that guys have that desire to work hard and win.

"Scotty was a great motivator, and he knew when he had to kick ass and when he had to ease off," said Houle. "And he had Piton [assistant coach Claude Ruel] there to calm things down if he went too far."

Houle said one of Bowman's strengths was developing game plans.

"He studied the opponents," said Houle. "He knew what to expect for every game. He knew the strengths and the weaknesses of the opponent, and we were prepared for every game we played. He was also a master at managing a game. He could tell when a player or a line was struggling, and he was able to make adjustments."

Bowman won his first Stanley Cup in 1973 and guided the Canadiens to four consecutive Stanley Cups from 1976 to 1979. Their dominance is reflected in the individual honors accorded the players:

Ken Dryden won the Vezina Trophy as the top goaltender five times; he won the Conn Smythe Trophy as the most valuable player in the 1971 playoffs, and, a year later, he won the Calder Trophy as the top rookie. No Canadien has won the rookie award since then.

Other Conn Smythe recipients in the decade were Yvan Cournoyer (1973), Guy Lafleur (1977), Larry Robinson (1978), and Bob Gainey (1979).

Guy Lafleur was a two-time winner of the Hart Trophy as most valuable player and a three-time winner of the Lester B. Pearson Award as the players' choice for MVP. He also took home the Art Ross Trophy as the NHL's leading scorer three times.

Larry Robinson won the Norris Trophy as the top defenseman. Henri Richard and Serge Savard won the Masterton Trophy for perseverance and dedication to the game.

Bob Gainey set the standard for defensive forwards, and the league created the Frank J. Selke Trophy to recognize this skill. Gainey won the inaugural award in 1978 and also won in each of the next three seasons.

Cournoyer, Gainey, Lafleur, Savard, Dryden, Henri Richard, Jacques Lemaire, Frank Mahovlich, Jean Béliveau, Jacques Laperriere, Guy Lapointe, Steve Shutt, and Dick Duff are all honored members of the Hockey Hall of Fame.

CHAPTER 2
THE LAST TIME

There are many factors that go into winning the Stanley Cup. Talent is a prerequisite, and it's a plus when your top players are peaking for the postseason.

It's time for unsung heroes to step up, and it's a definite advantage if your goaltender is on the road to the Hockey Hall of Fame.

There's also a matter of luck, and, in 1993, the Canadiens had to tip their hats to the Buffalo Sabres and the New York Islanders. The Sabres upset the Boston Bruins in the first round of the playoffs while the Islanders defeated the Pittsburgh Penguins, the heavily favored two-time defending champions, in the second round.

Road to the Cup Goes Through Quebec

There was a feeling of euphoria in Quebec City when the Nordiques finished in second place in the Adams Division, two points ahead of the rival Canadiens.

The finish gave the Nordiques their first playoff appearance since 1987, and team owner Marcel Aubut was determined to upstage the folks from the big city.

While Quebec City is the provincial capital, it is dwarfed by Montreal in terms of size and financial clout. Aubut was determined to show that Quebec could compete not only on the ice but also in other areas.

He scored a coup when he convinced Ginette Reno to sing the national anthem prior to the games at Le Colisée. It was an idea he borrowed from the Philadelphia Flyers, who had great success when they enlisted television star Kate Smith to sing "God Bless America" before important games.

Reno, who has been employed by the Canadiens in recent years to sing "O Canada" during the playoffs, was the biggest star in Quebec in 1993, and the Montreal native received a standing ovation when she appeared wearing the blue and white colors of the Nordiques.

Aubut also made an effort to win the hearts, minds—and stomachs—of the media. Reporters arriving for the pregame meal prior to Game 1 were greeted by two of Quebec City's top chefs serving lobsters, salmon, and filet mignon.

Aubut's crew didn't make as good an impression on the ice as Montreal goaltender Patrick Roy kept the home team off the scoreboard until Gilbert Dionne made a costly mistake. He took an elbowing penalty at 17:17 of the third period while the Canadiens were ahead 2–0. The Nordiques pulled goaltender Ron Hextall for a 6-on-4 advantage, and Martin Rucinsky scored with 1:29 remaining in regulation time.

Hextall remained on the bench and the extra attacker paid off again when Joe Sakic scored with 49 seconds left to send the game into overtime.

The Nordiques escaped with a win when Scott Young scored at 16:49 of overtime. Young skated down the right side and stepped around Montreal defenseman J.J. Daigneault. He continued around the Canadiens' net before surprising Roy with a wraparound.

"We had a good breakout," said Young. "Mike Ricci got me the puck, and I had some speed up. I went behind the net looking to pass, but I saw it was wide open and decided to try to stuff it in. It just trickled by Roy, and I'm not sure where it went in."

"It was a great feeling and a real emotional win, but we have to come down quickly," Young said. "We've got to rest and be ready for Tuesday."

Young and the Nordiques were ready for Game 2. Young scored twice as Quebec jumped out to a 3–0 lead and coasted to a 4–1 win. Hextall was outstanding as he stopped 32 of 33 shots while Roy let in a couple of goals, which were generously described as soft.

The Quebec City media had a field day as it critiqued Roy, who was born in suburban Sainte-Foy. One commentator suggested that the 27-year-old was over the hill and should retire. A newspaper trumpeted the win with the headline "Nordiques win game, battle of goaltenders" and a subhead that read "Hextall gets the better of Roy." Dan Bouchard, the Nordiques goaltending coach, piled on by saying the Nordiques had uncovered Roy's weaknesses. Radio talk shows called for head coach Jacques Demers to replace Roy with backup André Racicot, a journeyman who had been unfairly nicknamed Red Light.

All the talk had the effect of poking a sleeping bear because Roy and the Canadiens swept the next four games, although there were some anxious moments and two of the wins came in overtime.

When the series moved to the Montreal Forum for Game 3, it looked as if the game would follow the same script as the first two games. Mats Sundin gave Quebec a 1–0 lead when he scored at 1:17 of the first period on the third shot fired at Roy. Hextall continued to be outstanding, but Kirk Muller tied the game with a power-play goal in the second period.

Eight minutes into the overtime, the Canadiens thought they had a winning goal, but it was disallowed because Stéphan Lebeau's stick was clearly was over the height of the crossbar when he scored.

But Quebec's Curtis Leschyshyn opened the door when he took a slashing penalty at 9:26, and Vincent Damphousse scored the winning goal at 10:30 on a short backhander that was deflected in front. The Nordiques argued that Muller kicked the puck in, but a replay showed that the puck bounced off Quebec defenseman Alexei Gusarov.

"You could see we had it," said Brian Bellows, who assisted on Damphousse's goal. "They started pretty good, but we kept building up more and more steam. We had it in the overtime. It was so frustrating—all those chances. We finally got it done, though. We used a lot of players and got it done."

The Canadiens outshot the Nordiques 50–35 and 12 of the Montreal shots came from 10 different players in overtime. For the third consecutive game, Hextall was outstanding, but Roy showed that he was capable of making the difference.

The Canadiens tied the series at 2–2 when Benoit Brunet scored early in the third period, and the stage was set for another nail-biter at Le Colisée. This time around, offenses prevailed. Montreal won 5–4 on an overtime goal by Kirk Muller but not before some high drama involving Roy.

Mike Keane scored the only goal in the first period to give the Canadiens the lead, but the complexion of the game changed on the opening shift of the second period when Mike Hough unleashed a slap shot that struck Roy in the collarbone. The goaltender collapsed on the ice, but elected to stay in the game. But when Andrei Kovalenko scored 90 seconds later, it was obvious that Roy was in a world of hurt, and he skated to the bench.

While Roy was receiving medical attention, Racicot gave up two goals on nine shots, but the Canadiens scored twice. The score was tied 3–3 going into the third.

The Canadiens' medical staff injected Roy with a painkiller, but it didn't do the job. He insisted on a second injection and then went back to work. He gave up a goal to Sundin, but Gilbert Dionne beat Hextall and then set up the OT winner for Muller. The Nordiques dominated the extra period, outshooting Montreal 5–0 before the Canadiens countered with an odd-man rush. Damphousse found Muller on the right wing and scored on a slap shot when Hextall came out to cut down the angle. After four outstanding performances, Hextall was ordinary as he allowed five goals on 30 shots.

Hextall was less than ordinary two nights later as the Canadiens wrapped up the series with a 6–2 win at the Forum. Hextall was yanked in favour of Stéphane Fiset late in the second period after giving up five goals on 23 shots. Paul DiPietro, who spent half the season in the American Hockey League, had a hat trick for the Canadiens. The Sault Ste. Marie native had four goals in 29 regular-season games but scored eight times in 17 playoff games.

Shufflin' Off to Buffalo

The Boston Bruins finished the regular season with 109 points for the second-best record in the NHL, but they were surprised by the Buffalo Sabres in the opening round of the playoffs. The Sabres had slipped into the playoffs with 86 points, but they posted three overtime victories against the Bruins. Brad May scored the overtime winner in Game 4, and Buffalo broadcaster

Rick Jeanneret produced his classic May Day goal call. But it was the Canadiens who produced the overtime magic in the Adams Division final. They swept the Sabres, but the series couldn't have been closer. Each game ended in a 4–3 score, and the final three games went to overtime.

The Canadiens never trailed in Game 1, and Vincent Damphousse scored the winning goal at 6:50 of the third period after Buffalo scored twice in the second period to rally from a 3–1 deficit.

This series featured what was supposed to be a goaltending duel between Patrick Roy and Buffalo's Grant Fuhr, a future Hall of Famer who had won four Stanley Cups with the Edmonton Oilers. It was Roy who made the difference in Game 2. The Sabres outshot the Canadiens 31–25, but Fuhr was soft on the first two Montreal goals and captain Guy Carbonneau provided some inspirational words prior to the overtime and then scored the winning goal.

"I told the guys, 'You don't want to go to Buffalo 1–1,'" he said. "I told them, 'Maybe in a month you'll be sitting down having a beer and saying this is the one that was important—that this game, this shift was the most important of your career.'"

Carbonneau also told the Canadiens that this wasn't the time to be satisfied.

"We've played only good enough to win in these two games," he said, "and that's not good enough. We can't be satisfied with that—particularly since we're going into their rink."

The Canadiens made it 3–0 with another 4–3 overtime win in Buffalo. Gilbert Dionne was credited with the winning goal when a shot by Patrice Brisebois was deflected past Fuhr.

Dionne insisted that the shot went off his leg, but an ESPN replay showed that the puck went in off the Sabres Pat LaFontaine. That prompted Dionne to say: "ESPN should stick to baseball; they don't know hockey."

But Game 3 is remembered not for the win, but for a horrific accident that resulted in a broken leg for Sabres' star Alexander Mogilny. The Russian superstar had scored 76 goals in 77 regular-season games and was averaging a goal a game in the playoffs when he was injured trying to stop a rush by Brian Bellows.

Bellows, who returned to the lineup after missing the first two games with a cracked rib, was bearing down on Fuhr when Mogilny hooked him from behind. At the same time, Pat Lafontaine came from the right side and checked Bellows. The force knocked Bellows off stride and he fell into Mogilny with his weight coming down on the Russian's leg.

A hush fell over Buffalo's Memorial Auditorium, but the silence was broken by an anguished cry from Mogilny. The trainers rushed onto the ice, but it took several minutes to get Mogilny to his feet, and he was then helped off the ice by his teammates. X-rays revealed a broken fibula.

Buffalo went into Game 4 without Mogilny and without LaFontaine, but they managed to take the Canadiens to overtime before losing 4–3 on a goal by Kirk Muller. The goal allowed Muller to atone for messing up a 2-on-0 breakaway in the final minute of regulation time.

With Montreal leading 3–2, the Sabres pulled Fuhr for an extra attacker. That led to a break for Muller, and when he spotted Carbonneau joining the rush, he tried to play nice guy and feed the captain. But his pass took Carbonneau wide, and, by the time he took the shot from a wide angle, Donald Audette had caught up to the play and he made the save. That provided Yuri Khmylev with an opportunity to score the tying goal with fewer than 10 seconds remaining in regulation time.

"I really made a mistake," Muller said. "Those things usually come back to haunt you and this one almost did. Sometimes it pays to be selfish. I was just going down the ice and I saw Carbo, and I thought, 'Oh, he's open.' I wanted to give it to him. I didn't want to put it in the corner, obviously. It was a dumb play.

"Imagine screwing up a simple play like that," added Muller. "But I was tired, and I wanted to make sure I gained the red [line]. I should have taken another stride and let it go, but I wanted to give it to him for some reason. Maybe I should have had more of a killer instinct."

When my colleague Michael Farber asked Carbonneau if that was the worst pass he had ever received, he replied: "Probably, because if it had been to me, I would have scored and then I'd remember what happened in the game because it would have been over."

Carbonneau couldn't remember because he was hit in the head by a puck early in the overtime and suffered a possible concussion.

It was over when Muller scored at 11:37 of overtime, but the Sabres gave it their all. Buffalo outshot Montreal 12–9 in the overtime.

LaFontaine put the series in perspective when he said: "Usually when you think of a sweep, you think of a team that's been beat pretty good. Those were four 4–3 games that could have gone either way."

27

Penguins Sent Packing

Only a fool would have bet against the Pittsburgh Penguins heading into the 1993 playoffs. The Penguins finished with the best record in the NHL at 56–21–7, and their 119 points were 10 better than the Boston Bruins. The Penguins had won the Cup in 1991 and repeated in 1992 when they swept the Boston Bruins in the Eastern Conference Final and then swept the Chicago Blackhawks in the final.

Mario Lemieux led the league in scoring with 160 points, including 69 goals, despite missing 24 games with back problems and Hodgkin's disease. His supporting cast included a young Jaromir Jagr and fellow all-stars Larry Murphy, Kevin Stevens, and Tom Barrasso. Stevens, Rick Tocchet, and Ron Francis all joined Lemieux in the 100-point club. To top it off, the man behind the bench was Scotty Bowman, who had presided over the Canadiens' dynasty in the 1970s.

The Penguins opened the playoffs by beating the New Jersey Devils in five games, but they ran into a roadblock in the Islanders, who were a decade removed from the end of their own dynastic run.

The Islanders, who finished third in the Patrick Division with 87 points, upset Washington in six games but went into Pittsburgh without Pierre Turgeon, who had scored 132 points in the regular season. Turgeon suffered a shoulder injury when he was hit by Dale Hunter in Game 6 of the Washington series, a cheap shot that would result in 21-game suspension for Hunter.

The underdog Islanders shocked the Penguins and a sellout crowd in the Igloo by posting a 3–2 win in Game 1. The loss was compounded by Lemieux's departure from the game with what the Penguins described as back spasms.

Lemieux was scratched from Game 2 and said the problem was acute pain in his back, an aftereffect of surgery. But Lemieux's absence wasn't a problem as the Penguins were 3–0 winners behind a 26-save performance by Barrasso.

Lemieux returned for Game 3, and the Penguins regained the home-ice advantage with a 3–1 win.

The first three games of the series were tight-checking, low-scoring contests, and Game 4 started out in the same vein. It was 0–0 until Jagr scored at 13:12 of the second period to open the floodgates. Ten more goals were scored over the next 19 minutes, and Derek King's goal at 12:11 of the third period gave the Islanders a 6–5 win and tied the series at 2–2. Lemieux picked up an assist on a power-play goal by Kevin Stevens for his first point of the series.

There was nothing wrong with Lemieux's back in Game 5. He needed only 19 seconds to score his first goal of the series, and he picked up an assist on Rick Tocchet's goal at the 54-second mark. Larry Murphy made it 3–0 at 1:48, and the Islanders were hopelessly behind. Lemieux finished the game with two goals and an assist, and the 6–3 decision left the Penguins one win away from advancing to the conference final.

Game 6 was another nightmare for goaltenders Barrasso and Glenn Healy. This time, it was the Islanders who struck early with Brad Dalgarno scoring at the 25-second mark, but the score seesawed throughout with New York winning 7–5. Lemieux had another goal and Stevens scored twice, but Steve Thomas made the difference with two goals, including the game-winner.

The deciding game was back at the Civic Arena in Pittsburgh, and the Penguins offense was firing on all cylinders as they outshot the Islanders 45–20.

Unfortunately, this was not Barrasso's finest moment. While Healy was stopping 42 shots, including seven from Lemieux, Barrasso struggled. The teams were tied 3–3 at the end of regulation time, and the overtime winner came from an unlikely source, Czech David Volek.

The previous summer, Volek had been involved in a contract dispute with Islanders general manager Bill Torrey. When there was little progress made on a new deal, Torrey let it be known that he was willing to trade Volek. Eventually, the two sides worked out a deal but the 1992–93 season was not a happy one for Volek. He played only 56 games and scored eight goals. At one point, he was a healthy scratch for 18 consecutive games.

He watched the Washington series from the press box, and he didn't see any playoff action until Game 3 of the Penguins series. But he proved his worth in Game 7, scoring once in regulation and then notching the winner on a 2-on-1 break with Ray Ferraro.

The magic was short-lived. Volek played one more unproductive season in the NHL before going home.

Push to the Final

Sweeping the Sabres gave the Canadiens a week's rest before they faced the New York Islanders in the Eastern Conference Final, but coach Jacques Demers wasn't going to let his charges grow complacent as they waited for the Islanders to beat the Penguins.

Patrick Roy deflects a first period shot against the Islanders during Game 4 of the Conference Finals. *(AP Photo/Bob Child)*

"It wasn't anything one-on-one, he talked to the team in general and said it was up to the guys to sorta, kinda jump on the stuff and know when he was talking to them," said John LeClair. "Like I knew he was talking to me when he mentioned some of the guys hadn't shown much."

LeClair, who grew up down the road from Montreal in St. Albans, Vermont, took Demers's words to heart in Game 1 of the Islanders series. He scored two goals as the Canadiens thrashed the Islanders 4–1.

It was a good start to the series, but LeClair knew the Islanders were physically and emotionally drained after their surprise win over the Penguins.

"The rest of the series isn't going to be easy," said LeClair, and he was right.

The fabled Forum Ghosts had to work overtime to ensure a 4–3 win in Game 2. The Islanders led with five minutes to play in regulation, but Paul DiPietro tied the game. Diminutive Stéphan Lebeau scored his second goal of the game at 6:21 of the second overtime period.

Lebeau had missed the Sabres series because of an injury and was one of the players who benefitted from the time off between games.

"Steph's not very big, but he plays with a big heart," said Vincent Damphousse, who set up Lebeau for the winning goal. "He's been in and out of the lineup for the past six weeks because he's been hurt, and he's still hurt, but he came through tonight."

Lebeau, who was coming off his most productive NHL season with 31 goals and 80 points in 71 games, was listed at 5 foot 10, but he was several inches shorter. He was a scoring machine in junior hockey but might not have had a chance at the pros if Ron Lapointe, his junior coach with the Shawinigan Cataractes, hadn't resorted to some sleight of hand.

When the Canadiens sent a scout to measure Lebeau, Lapointe claimed he taped pucks to the player's feet and had him wear several pairs of socks to boost his weight. He also had Lebeau put lead weights in his sweats to push his weight over 170 pounds.

There was more overtime magic in Game 3, and after Guy Carbonneau scored at 12:34 of overtime to give the Canadiens a 2–1 victory, there was a lot of talk about the Canadiens being a team of destiny. The Islanders outplayed Montreal for most of the game, but Damphousse scored late in the third period to tie the game.

It was the Canadiens' 11th consecutive win and their seventh win in eight overtime encounters.

The winning streak came to an end in Game 4 as the Islanders won 4–1 at Nassau Coliseum.

"They played a perfect game," Demers said. "Everybody was talking sweep. It's not a sweep. As we recall, they beat the Pittsburgh Penguins. We knew they were tough. The Islanders didn't want to lose in front of their fans. You could sense that. They were ready in warm-ups. It started right there. They threw everything at us.

"It's been a great ride," Demers said. "A lot of fun but also a lot of pressure. We just gave them a little bit of life, maybe more than a little bit."

Nah.

Patrick Roy stopped 26 shots to lead the Canadiens to a series-clinching 5–2 win at the Forum, and he gave the Canadiens' final-round opponent something to think about when he said he was playing better than he was in 1986 when he led Montreal to the Stanley Cup with a 15–5 record and 1.92 goals against average as a rookie. He was rewarded with the Conn Smythe Trophy as the most valuable player in those playoffs.

Through the first three rounds of the playoffs, Roy had a 12–3 record with a 2.33 GAA.

"I'm very sharp right now," Roy said after locking up the Eastern Conference Final. "I think I'm playing better than in '86.

"This has been a great team effort," Roy added. "Everyone was sharp. Guys were taking cheap shots and didn't retaliate; they took it for the team. We played against three great teams in the playoffs, so for us to beat them we had to play really well."

Sticking It to the Kings

The Stanley Cup Final matched a pair of teams that finished sixth in their respective conferences in the regular season. Wayne Gretzky led the Los Angeles Kings' improbable run to the final with upset series wins over Calgary, Vancouver, and Toronto. Television executives at the CBC had been rooting for a Montreal-Toronto final but having The Great One in the house was an attractive consolation prize.

Gretzky was full value in the opening game on June 1 as the Kings shocked the Canadiens and a standing-room-only crowd at the Forum with a 4–1 victory. Gretzky scored a goal and also assisted on a pair of goals by Luc Robitaille and another by Jari Kurri. Kelly Hrudey was outstanding as he stopped 31 Montreal shots, and there was a feeling that the magic had run out for the Canadiens.

That feeling was reinforced two nights later when the Kings carried a 2–1 lead into the final two minutes of the game. That's when Montreal coach Jacques Demers pulled an ace out of his sleeve and asked referee Kerry Fraser to measure defenseman Marty McSorley's stick.

The measurement showed that the curve of the blade exceeded the half-inch allowable maximum and McSorley was sent to the penalty box at 18:15. Demers pulled goaltender Patrick Roy to give Montreal a 6-on-4 advantage, and defenseman Eric Desjardins scored at 18:47 to send the game into overtime. Desjardins scored his third goal of the game at the 51-second mark of overtime, and the series was suddenly tied 1–1. Desjardins' hat trick was overshadowed by the illegal stick call, but he is the only defenseman in NHL history to score three goals in a Stanley Cup Final game.

Jacques Demers lifts the Stanley Cup above his head on June 6, 1993, to win the Canadiens' 23rd NHL championship. *(AP Photo/Jacques Boissinot)*

After the game, McSorley admitted he made a mistake, but the defenseman added he wasn't going to lose any sleep over it. "I made a mistake but all I can do now is play hockey," said McSorley.

McSorley's penalty was the prime topic of conversation among the Kings after the loss. Nobody came out and said it, but the undercurrent suggested that the Kings thought the call for a measurement was a chintzy decision by Demers.

Kings coach Barry Melrose talked about the respect he has for Demers but went on to say that he wouldn't call for a measurement because "I don't believe in winning that way."

When asked if he was surprised that Demers called for the measurement, Melrose said: "No. This is a pressure-packed place to play. Pressure breeds things like that."

"You do what you have to do to win," McSorley said when asked for his opinion of the call. "I'm a veteran. I should have known better. I always have one stick in the rack that I absolutely know is legal, but I guess I got caught up in the emotion of the game and I grabbed the wrong one."

The stick, a USA model made by the Christian brothers of Minnesota, had a curve exceeding the half-inch maximum.

"I was playing with some new sticks that I got earlier today," said McSorley, who disputed Demers' claim that the Canadiens first spotted his illegal stick prior to Game 1 of the series. "Some of them had a bigger curve than I like, and I put the torch to them. I should have checked and shaved it down a bit."

McSorley, who said he had never been called for a stick violation before, said he would heed Melrose's order to check all his sticks prior to Game 3. Melrose had his tongue in cheek when he suggested that his players would all check the length of their sticks "and the length of the bootlaces" before Game 3.

"I was surprised when they asked for my stick," McSorley said. "I was talking to [goaltender Kelly Hrudey] and getting ready for a faceoff in our end when they asked for it. I was concentrating on the game because we were up 2–1 and we just had to hold them off another 1:45. But even then, I talked to [Wayne Gretzky] and told him I thought my stick was okay."

"It's unfortunate that it happened to a guy who plays as hard as Marty," Gretzky said. "I don't think there's another guy who wants to win as much as he does."

"He's probably not the only guy on this team with an illegal stick or two," fellow defenseman Rob Blake said. "I think Marty probably feels bad about this, but we know how we played tonight, and we played well enough to win."

The controversy over the stick didn't end that night. While Demers insisted that captain Guy Carbonneau tipped him off about the illegal curve, McSorley and the Kings believed that the Canadiens received some inside information from a Forum employee.

In a 2017 interview with NHL.com, McSorley said the Canadiens knew he had an illegal stick because they had inside information.

"I think that Barry Melrose, Luc Robitaille, [former trainer] Peter Demers, different guys, have basically said what happened. We all know they pulled the stick rack into their locker room. That's honest and that's frank. Am I sitting here complaining? No. But that is what happened."

Melrose was in fine form as the series moved to the Great Western Forum for Games 3 and 4. He held court for nearly an hour on the eve of the third game and made light of the stick incident.

"I read the rulebook today and found we have two urinals in our bathroom that are four inches too high," he said.

When asked if he was concerned about the Canadiens' mystique, Melrose said: "No, the French eat that up. History's nice to look at, but you can't live in it."

When told that the Canadiens might have an advantage because they didn't travel outside of their time zone in the first three series, Melrose grinned and said: "Well, that's not fair because Montreal had those tough one-hour trips to New York there in that last series."

Melrose did get serious when he was asked about the defensive play of Guy Carbonneau, who kept Gretzky off the scoreboard in Game 2.

"They're making a big deal of the job they did on him," replied Melrose. "I don't think that they're mentioning that Wayne had three two-on-ones and almost set Tomas [Sandstrom] up for a clear-cut breakaway. So he didn't score or get an assist, but he easily could have four points. They didn't do that great a job against him, and now I'll be able to keep him away from Carbonneau in this building a bit.

"You start saying stuff like that to Wayne, it just fuels him," added Melrose. "I hope they talk about that for the next two days, what a great job they did on him."

Gretzky did respond in Game 3 with a goal and assist as the Kings rebounded from a 0–3 deficit to force the game into overtime. But overtime wasn't a place you wanted to be with the Canadiens in these playoffs, and it took only 34 seconds for

John LeClair to give Montreal a 4–3 win. More than 18,000 fans donated $2 each to Montreal's children's hospitals to watch the game on the scoreboard screen at the Forum.

Kirk Muller and Vincent Damphousse gave Montreal the lead in Game 4, and again the Kings came back to force overtime. And again LeClair delivered the winner. His goal at 14:37 provided Montreal with a record 10th overtime win, and the Canadiens were heading home with a 3–1 series lead.

"I'm sitting here not really knowing what to say," Carbonneau said after the game, "but what I do know is that Patrick [Roy] came into the dressing room after the second period and said that was the last goal he was giving up. He kept his promise."

So did LeClair, who came into the room after the third period and yelled: "Let's go, guys. I've got lots left."

"What can you say about that guy," said Carbonneau. "He's finally learning how good he can be. He's finally learning how to get things done with his size. He said he had lots left. We need guys that size to do the job for us."

The Kings were a dispirited group when they returned to Montreal for Game 5. The three overtime losses had taken their toll, and, when the team bus arrived after the cross-continent flight, the players passed silently through the lobby of the Loew's Hotel Vogue, picked up their keys, and headed to their rooms.

There were a half-dozen reporters in the lobby looking for a story, but the Kings' public relations personnel said no players were available. The media conferred with NHL officials, and, after 30 minutes of negotiations, the Kings said Melrose would address the reporters.

It was a far cry from his press conference between Games 3 and 4. On that occasion, he entertained the media for close to two hours.

This time around, Melrose tried to be upbeat, but his body language said he didn't want to be there. He talked about how fatigue would finally get to the Canadiens in Game 6 although there was no guarantee there would be a Game 6.

"We're playing good hockey," said Melrose. "In the game last night, we outworked them. Our guys did exactly what I wanted them to do in the overtime. They attacked, they played aggressive hockey. But it was a bounce here, a bounce there."

Those bounces added up to three consecutive overtime wins for Montreal, and Melrose said it's not difficult to pinpoint the difference to this point.

"Patrick Roy is playing excellent hockey," said Melrose. "Our guy, Kelly Hrudey, is also playing well, and we wouldn't be where we are without him. But the Canadiens wouldn't be here without Roy. Look back to the Quebec series and you see what happens when Roy isn't playing his best. He didn't play well the first two games and the Nordiques won."

"Last night, he made four or five outstanding saves in the overtime," said Melrose. "We were getting the shots from the guys we wanted to shoot. Gretz [Wayne Gretzky] had a good chance and [Tomas] Sandstrom had one and so did [Tony] Granato. But Roy made the saves. I think we had a 10–3 edge in shots at one point."

When asked what it would it take to beat Roy, Melrose replied: "One more goal than they score."

Melrose was quick to point out that he wasn't concerned about the Forum Ghosts or being beaten by some memory.

"That's an insult to Jacques Demers and his team," said Melrose. "I know that if I had my team up 3–1 in the Stanley Cup Final and someone was giving the credit to Toe Blake, I'd be pretty pissed off."

There would be no Game 6.

Paul DiPietro scored two goals, Kirk Muller provided the game-winner, and Roy—who won his second Conn Smythe Trophy as the playoff MVP—didn't have to be at his best because the Kings managed only 19 shots on goal. The Canadiens took a 2–1 lead and coasted to a 4–1 victory.

"I had a feeling that we were going to score one way or another on that play," said Muller, who was in the slot in front of Hrudey when he took a pass from Damphousse and flipped a shot into the top corner.

"Earlier in the playoffs, the other teams were taking that away from us," Muller said. "We started working more behind the net, and it opened things up for us. On the goal tonight, Vinny made a good move shaking his check behind the net. I knew that he was either going to wrap it around and I had a chance for a rebound if he missed or he would pass it out. He got the pass to me, and I had plenty of time."

Muller said winning the Stanley Cup was a greater thrill than he could have imagined.

"It was nine years coming, and I can't describe what it means," Muller said as he drained a bottle of Evian water to fight off dehydration in the hot and crowded Montreal dressing room. "All I've ever wanted was one shot at it, and we got it this year. I feel great for the older guys like Brian [Bellows], Denis [Savard], guys who may not get another chance at it."

Muller, who spent seven years in New Jersey before being traded to the Canadiens in 1991, said the victory was the result of "25 or 26 guys who were willing to pay the price. We have a good balance of young guys and veterans, and we all came together. I've never played on a team as close as this one."

The closeness extended to the postgame celebrations as the players celebrated along with their families.

"I think we all want to be together," said John LeClair, who represented the youth wing of the Canadiens. LeClair, who scored overtime winners in Games 3 and 4, had two assists in the final game.

"That's one of the great things about this team," LeClair said. "We have a lot of guys who are capable of chipping in. Kirk came through with a big goal tonight, but we also got two big goals from Paulie [DiPietro].

"People don't realize we have a pretty young team," LeClair added. "Tonight we're going to celebrate, but sometime next week we'll start to think about next year."

Panic in the Streets

While the Canadiens were celebrating in the Forum locker room, there was a different kind of celebration going on in the streets.

As we sat in the press box writing our game stories, we started hearing horror stories about a celebration gone bad.

As I started to leave the building shortly before midnight, one of the Forum security guards urged me to be careful and suggested that I head west, away from the downtown core.

Ignoring the advice, I headed down Ste. Catherine Street, the main drag, and found myself travelling in the path of a mob that left broken shop windows and vandalized cars and buses in its wake.

Despite a heavy police presence in the streets surrounding the Forum, delirious fans went on a rampage, smashing store windows and tossing beer bottles and other objects.

There was at least one overturned police cruiser and numerous cars with their side mirrors ripped off. The sidewalks and streets were littered with broken glass.

Montreal Urban Community police said they had deployed about four times the number of officers and patrol vehicles in the area surrounding the Forum than they would normally send to a hockey game.

Although the fans started climbing onto light standards and smashed at least one Forum window seconds after the Canadiens clinched the Cup, police appeared hesitant to move in right away. Riot police could be seen on a side street putting on equipment 30 minutes after the game had ended.

The first signs of violence occurred at 10:35 PM. About 50 revellers stormed a 24-hour convenience store three blocks from the Forum. They threw bottles of beer, smashing the store window. They grabbed cases of beer and bottles of soda pop while stunned cashiers stood helplessly behind the counter.

Police arrived on the scene 10 minutes later. Customers inside the store emerged with metal baskets protecting their heads.

As police stood guard at the store entrance, bottles flew through the air. Fights broke out between revellers, and police were seen arresting four young men.

Delirious fans started crowding Ste. Catherine Street halfway through the final period of the game, scattering firecrackers and throwing rolls of toilet paper through the air. At 11:00 PM, 30 riot police marched in front of Faubourg Ste. Catherine shopping center and stood guard.

The problems weren't unexpected. In 1986, when Montreal won its last Stanley Cup on the road in Calgary, about 5,000 to 10,000 fans rampaged along Ste. Catherine smashing windows, looting stores, and setting cars on fire.

With 18,000 fans already downtown attending the Cup-clinching home game, police knew they'd have their hands full and took extra precautions to prevent problems.

As was the case following the Canadiens' Game 4 victory in Los Angeles—which sent thousands of fans parading on Ste. Catherine Street—there were police officers positioned at every block leading from the Forum to the downtown core.

When Stéphan Lebeau scored midway through the second period to put the Canadiens up 3–1, fans began trickling out of bars on nearby Crescent and Bishop Streets to congregate near the Forum for the anticipated celebration.

The cheers of the crowd were punctuated by sirens from police cruisers and ambulances. Police arrested 115 people, and 168 injuries were reported. It was well after 2:00 AM when some semblance of order was restored to the city.

While city workers and shopkeepers swept up broken glass and took stock of stolen merchandise the next morning, an angry Mayor Jean Doré said police are going to have to get tough with people who turn celebrations into orgies of looting.

Doré said much of the looting was carried out by organized gangs. But many merchants blamed the Montreal Urban Community police for failing to control the thousands of revellers who took over Ste. Catherine Street in the three-mile stretch between Atwater Avenue and St. Hubert Street.

By the time the downtown core had been cleared by phalanxes of helmeted police officers moving through the streets a few feet at a time, 100 stores on Ste. Catherine Street had been ransacked, six fires set, and damage done to 15 buses, three Metro cars, and 47 police cars.

Property damage and losses were estimated at $10 million by the Insurance Board of Canada.

A spokesman for the city's public works department said the cost just for the city of Montreal will be "tens of thousands" of dollars—$25,000 alone for city equipment wrecked by rioters.

Store manager Arthur Auerbach said police should have learned a lesson from the riot that followed the Stanley Cup victory in 1986.

"They just weren't prepared," Auerbach told the *Montreal Gazette* as he surveyed the damage at La Boutique de Jeans A & B. "Look at my store. There's more than $20,000 worth of clothes stolen. It looks like a tornado hit it—Hurricane Jean Doré."

The timing of the riot was ironic for police chief Alain St. Germain, who was planning to retire later in the month. St. Germain began his career in 1954 and was one of the officers involved in the infamous Richard Riot. Now, he was dealing with another hockey riot as his career was ending.

St. Germain said the police were in a Catch-22 situation. He noted that 1,500 of the estimated 15,000 people in the street were there to cause trouble.

"We took measures we thought were appropriate," said St. Germain. "But you will understand that right now there are people who have no respect for life or property and these people were organized in advance to start trouble."

St. Germain said there were about 650 police officers in the downtown core when the game ended shortly after 10:00 PM. By midnight, that number had increased to 980, but one frustrated officer told reporters that the police were overwhelmed by the number of people on the street.

"I don't think we would have done better even if we had twice as many officers on the scene," St. German said at a news conference. "Even with twice the response, there would have been confrontations with the police. Our actions are linked to a social contract that requires the public to cooperate with its police department. Last night, a part of the population breached that contract."

Doré said that much of the violence could be attributed to organized gangs that used the celebration as a cover for their nefarious activities. Witnesses reported thieves carrying steel bars and bricks to smash windows. They said many of the thieves had garbage bags or pillowcases stuffed into their waistbands.

There was one report of a middle-aged man barking out orders to a group of teenagers as they ransacked a store.

The violence caused the Canadiens and the city to revise plans for the Stanley Cup parade and a block party that was to follow. The parade was shortened and the party was canceled.

The Canadiens did have a party a few days later. The 650 permanent employees of the team and the Forum gathered at the Queen Elizabeth Hotel to celebrate the win.

The party was an autograph-hunter's dream come true. In addition to members of the winning team, the guest list included legends Jean Béliveau, Jacques Lemaire, Jacques Laperriere, Serge Savard, and Yvan Cournoyer. Mona Savard, the wife of Denis Savard, took the microphone to sing, but the showstopper was megastar Céline Dion, who dedicated the song "Endless Love" to the Canadiens.

CHAPTER 3
DASHED HOPES

A fter the victory in 1993, there were hopes that the team was on the verge of another dynasty because the Canadiens' brightest stars were young.

Goaltender Patrick Roy was only 27. Vincent Damphousse, who was coming off a 97-point season, was 25, and Kirk Muller was 26. John LeClair, who had grown in stature during the play-offs, was 23, and Gilbert Dionne was 22.

And then there was the defense. Jean-Jacques Daigneault was the old man in the group at 27. Lyle Odelein was 24 while Mathieu Schneder and Eric Desjardins were 23. Sean Hill, Kevin Haller, and Patrice Brisebois were 22.

Denis Savard at 31 and Guy Carbonneau at 32 were the only regulars over the age of 28.

By the start of the 1995–96 season, only six players remained from the team that won the Stanley Cup three years earlier.

"They traded away many of the players, but, more importantly, they traded away the leaders," said former GM Serge Savard.

In the quarter century since their last Stanley Cup, the Canadiens have never advanced past the Eastern Conference Final. In that span, they have missed the playoffs nine times and they have reached the conference final twice. On three occasions, they were eliminated by teams that went on to win the Stanley Cup. In this chapter, we look at some of the seasons that ended in disappointment.

The Captain Goes Down

The Canadiens were underdogs when they headed to Carolina for the start of the 2006 playoffs. The Hurricanes finished first in the Southeast Division with 112 points while the Canadiens finished third in the Northeast Division. Carolina had won all four regular-season meetings.

There was a festive atmosphere surrounding Game 1 in Raleigh. The parking lots surrounding the RBC Centre were filled with tailgaters who took advantage of a warm spring day to set up charcoal grills and smokers. The scent of barbecued pork filled the air, and fans slaked their thirst with longneck bottles of beer while listening to a rock band performing on the plaza outside the arena.

The noise from the sellout crowd was deafening when Matt Cullen beat Cristobal Huet at the 50-second mark of the first period. But the fans wouldn't have many more reasons to cheer. Francis Bouillon tied the score at 8:23 and Radek Bonk put the Canadiens ahead at 16:17. Before it was over, Alex Kovalev would score twice with Chris Higgins and Sheldon Souray adding singles.

But the story of the game was the goaltending. Carolina outshot Montreal by a better than 2-to-1 margin, but Cristobal Huet stopped 42 of 43 shots while Martin Gerber gave up six goals on 21 shots.

There were questions as to whether Gerber would start Game 2, but Carolina coach Peter Laviolette noted Gerber had brought the team that far and he didn't plan a change. He probably thought he didn't have a choice because the alternative was Cam Ward, a 22-year-old rookie. Ward had appeared in 28 NHL games, but he had a 3.68 goals against average and a .882 save percentage.

Gerber wasn't any better in Game 2. The Hurricanes fell behind 3–0 as Gerber gave up goals to Jan Bulis, Michael Ryder, and Bonk before he was yanked at 14:46 of the first period. Ward held the fort long enough for Carolina to take a 4–3 lead, but the Canadiens jumped back into the lead at 5–4 before Cory Stillman's goal at 18:30 of the third period sent the game into overtime.

Montreal won 6–5 when Michael Ryder scored his second goal of the game at 2:32 of the second overtime period, and the Canadiens headed home with a 2–0 lead in the series and the prospect of facing a rookie goaltender the rest of the way. The Hurricanes announced that Gerber was suffering from a virus but would be available as Ward's backup.

Game 3 started out well for Montreal when Richard Zednik scored in the first period, but the series changed dramatically when captain Saku Koivu suffered a serious eye injury early in the second period.

Koivu was going hard to the net to catch up to a pass when Justin Williams attempted to lift his stick. Williams' blade went under Koivu's visor, and Koivu had bleeding under his left eye as he was helped off the ice.

Huet turned in another strong performance in Game 3, but it was Ward who emerged as the hero. He stopped 27 of 28 shots as the Hurricanes won 2–1 in overtime. Rod Brind'Amour tied the game in the second period, and Eric Staal scored the winner at 3:38 of overtime.

Nobody underestimated the importance of the Koivu injury, particularly Williams.

"Obviously, I hit him with a high stick," said Williams, who was mobbed by reporters when he appeared in Carolina's dressing room the day after the incident. "I put in a phone call to Saku this morning to tell him how I felt and say I hope he gets better. He's their heart and soul and their captain, so it's obviously a big loss for them."

"Saku is in the process of having some testing done to discern if or what damage has taken place," said Bob Gainey, who had replaced Claude Julien as head coach midseason. "Some of these can't be carried out for the next two to three days until some of the swelling subsides. He'll be unavailable to our team for an indefinite period."

Asked to speculate on the seriousness of Koivu's injury, Gainey did not sugarcoat his response.

"I'm working from the information I have and also that it's an eye, where you work from the worst-case scenario and work backwards," Gainey said.

The worst-case scenario was that Koivu's season was over.

"There's a million things we're going to miss about him," defenseman Sheldon Souray said. "He's our captain and leader, he's excellent on the power play. But we want to change the focus a bit and put it on the team. We still are in a good situation with a chance to win the next game at home."

It didn't work out that way.

Willlams scored a goal and added an assist and Brind'Amour scored the winner in the third period as Carolina evened the series 2–2.

Back in Raleigh, the Hurricanes posted a 2–1 win as Staal and Cullen scored power-play goals to back a 30-save performance by Ward. And the goaltender came through again as Carolina closed out the series with a 2–1 overtime win at the Bell Centre. Ward made 25 saves, and Stillman scored the winning goal.

The Hurricanes would go on to win the Stanley Cup, and Ward finished with 15 wins—Gerber shut out Buffalo in Game 4 of the Eastern Conference Final—and won the Conn Smythe Trophy as the playoff MVP. He was the first rookie goaltender to win the Cup since the Canadiens' Patrick Roy in 1986 and the first rookie goaltender to win the Conn Smythe Trophy since Philadelphia's Ron Hextall stood out in a losing cause against Edmonton in 1987.

Koivu, who had already bounced back from various knee injuries and a bout with cancer, was limited to two weeks training in the summer because of the eye injury, and the eye was red and partially closed when he showed up at the Canadiens' golf tournament in September.

Saku Koivu speaks to the media for the first time since taking a high stick to the eye from Justin Williams. (AP Photo/Ryan Remiorz, CP)

The veteran captain said he was experiencing problems with his peripheral vision and his eyesight would never be the same. But he expressed optimism that he would be ready to start the season. He was in the lineup for the season opener on October 6 in Buffalo and scored two goals and added an assist. He missed only one game in the 2006–07 season and was Montreal's leading scorer with 22 goals and 53 assists.

Leighton Returns to Haunt Habs

Michael Leighton's career with the Canadiens wasn't significant enough to be described as a footnote.

The Canadiens claimed him on waivers from the Philadelphia Flyers on February 27, 2007. He spent the remainder of the season in Montreal, but there's no mention of him in the Canadiens media guide. He's not listed in the all-time roster, nor will you find him in the all-time roster by number.

That's because Leighton never played a game for the Canadiens. They picked him up as insurance after Cristobal Huet suffered a season-ending hamstring injury, but he spent the final six weeks of the season watching David Aebischer and Jaroslav Halak.

Montreal was Leighton's sixth team in the 2006–07 season, and his new teammates kidded him about his travels.

"The guys told me I should put Velcro on the front of my practice jersey," Leighton recalled, grinning. "That way, I could tear off the crest and add a different one every other week."

He started the season with the Anaheim Ducks, went to their AHL farm club in Portland, Maine, and on to the Nashville

Predators, to Philadelphia (the Flyers and their AHL Phantoms), and finally to the Canadiens.

He didn't stay anywhere long enough to customize a helmet. He started wearing a plain white helmet when he went to Nashville. He decorated it with Predators logos, replaced them with Flyers logos in Philly, and finished the season with Canadiens stickers.

When the season ended, the Canadiens traded Leighton to Carolina for a seventh-round draft pick.

Leighton was far more visible when he returned to Montreal for the 2010 Eastern Conference Final as the starting goaltender for the Philadelphia Flyers. He was pressed into service when Brian Boucher was injured midway through the Eastern Conference semifinals, and he was solid as he led the Flyers back from a 0–3 deficit against Boston.

The Canadiens-Flyers series was an improbable conference final between the seventh and eighth seeds. Each team finished the regular season with 88 points, and the Flyers earned the home-ice advantage because they had more wins.

This was the year Jaroslav Halak stood on his head in the playoffs as the Canadiens upset the Washington Capitals in the first round in seven games and then beat the defending Stanley Cup–champion Pittsburgh Penguins in another seven-game series.

But it didn't matter what Halak did in the conference final because Leighton played the best hockey of his life. The Canadiens were eliminated in five games and Leighton shut them out in three of those games.

The Flyers lost to Chicago in the Cup Final, but Leighton finished the playoffs as the top goaltender with a 2.46 goals against average in 14 games. He hoped that the strong performance would end his days as a nomad, but it didn't happen. Over the next three seasons, he played only two games for the Flyers. He has since played one game with Chicago and four with Carolina.

Hopes Go Down with Price

To fully appreciate Carey Price's value to the Canadiens, you have to look at the team's performance when he's not in the lineup.

A case in point was the Canadiens' run to the Eastern Conference Final in 2014. The Canadiens had finished third in the Atlantic Division and were matched against the Tampa Bay Lightning, who also relied on a star goaltender in Ben Bishop. The Lightning finished one point ahead of the Canadiens in the standings, and the difference was their regular-season meetings. The Lightning won three of the four games, and Bishop limited the Canadiens to five goals.

The Lightning literally suffered a bad break when Ben Bishop fell during an April 8 game and injured his left wrist. Two days later, Tampa coach Jon Cooper said Bishop would miss the playoffs, but he expressed confidence in backup Anders Lindback.

The Swede finished the regular season in style. He stopped 25 shots after Bishop was injured in the Toronto game; he made 34 saves in a 4–2 win over Philadelphia and another 18 in a 1–0 overtime win over Washington.

Those numbers meant little in the playoffs. The Canadiens swept Tampa Bay because Price was good and Lindback wasn't, finishing with a 3.91 goals against average and a .881 save percentage.

Next up were the Boston Bruins, who had reached the Stanley Cup Final the previous year. This series went seven games as the Canadiens won the final two games behind two strong performances from Price. He made 26 saves as the Canadiens forced a Game 7 with a 4–0 win at the Bell Centre, and he followed that with a 29-save performance as the Canadiens won the deciding game at TD Garden 3–1.

The series ended on a bizarre note. As the players lined up for the traditional handshake after Game 7, the Bruins' Milan Lucic reportedly threatened Dale Weise and Alexei Emelin.

Television replays recorded the tension as Lucic aggressively shook hands with the Montreal players and paused as he confronted Weise and Emelin.

"Milan Lucic had a few things to say to a couple of guys," said Weise, who declined to go into specifics. "You look at a guy like Shawn Thornton who has been around the league and he plays hard and he plays that role and he had good things to say to everybody. He won with class and Milan Lucic just couldn't do that. Well, I won't get into what he said, it's just a poor way to lose."

The Bruin reportedly said: "I'm going to kill you next year," with an F-bomb thrown in for good measure.

An emotional Lucic wouldn't discuss the incident.

"It's said on the ice so it'll stay on the ice. So if he [Weise] wants to be a baby about it—he can make it public."

Next up were the New York Rangers, and any chance the Canadiens had to win the series disappeared when Chris Kreider crashed into Carey Price in the second period of Game 1 at the Bell Centre.

With the Rangers leading 2–0, Kreider went full speed on a breakaway with two Canadiens in close pursuit, lost his footing, and flew skates-first into Price.

Hockey Night in Canada clocked the collision at 22.6 miles an hour. Price winced in pain at the hit and appeared to have injured his right leg. After a short stoppage to test his leg, he said he was okay to continue. He gave up two more goals, including one to Kreider, and Peter Budaj replaced him for the third period.

Coach Michel Therrien said he replaced Price because the Canadiens weren't playing well in front of him. He gave Kreider the benefit of the doubt and described the collision as accidental.

The 23-year-old Kreider had a history of running into goaltenders and collided with Pittsburgh's Marc-André Fleury in the second round of the playoffs. He pleaded innocence on the Price hit.

"I had my head down trying to settle the puck," he said. "I put it wide and somehow lost my footing. I thought maybe someone pressured me from behind. I seem to have an issue staying on my feet on those, but then I went in skates-first, and I just had too much momentum and couldn't really avoid him."

The day after the collision, the Canadiens announced that Price was out for the remainder of the playoffs, and the rhetoric changed.

Brandon Prust, a former Ranger who slashed and speared Kreider, resulting in a double minor and a 10-minute misconduct later in Game 1, said: "I don't think Kreider ran him, but he didn't do anything to avoid him. Whether it's on purpose or accidental, he ran him pretty hard, and everybody thinks it was accidental, but we call it accidentally on purpose."

"The guy's lightning fast," Dale Weise said. "He's big, he's strong, he doesn't go easy. I think he's going so fast there. He's kind of like a deer in headlights. He had to pull up quick. I don't think there's anything wrong with it."

But Therrien touched off a war of words with his longtime rival and off-ice friend Alain Vigneault when he said: "Put it this way, he didn't make much effort to avoid the contact."

As the news sunk in that the Canadiens would not be getting Price back in the lineup, Therrien called the hit "a reckless play."

"That's the truth," said Therrien. "And Kreider, this is not the first time that he is going at goalies. We end up losing our best player, but our group has faced a lot of adversity through the course of the season, and we responded, and we had the attitude to respond really well. And that's what I'm expecting, starting tonight."

Therrien made a bold decision going into Game 2. He decided to start Dustin Tokarski, who played most of the season with the Hamilton Bulldogs in the AHL. Tokarski had been called up when Price took time off to deal with a knee injury after leading Canada to a gold medal at the Sochi Olympics. He posted a 2–0 record and had a 1.84 goals against average and Therrien decided to gamble.

Tokarski had a decent game in his first NHL playoff appearance, stopping 27 of 30 shots. Henrik Lundqvist, who has rarely played well at the Bell Centre in the regular season, gave up the first goal of the game to Max Pacioretty, but he finished with 40 saves in a 3–1 Rangers win.

The teams split 3–2 overtime decisions at Madison Square Garden to give New York a 3–1 lead in the series. When the series returned to Montreal for Game 5, the Canadiens delivered a performance that was guaranteed to give Therrien ulcers.

Tokarski was bad, but Lundqvist was worse. The Rangers goaltender was yanked at 6:54 of the second period after giving up four goals on 19 shots. His replacement, Cam Talbot, held the fort long enough for the Rangers to rally from a 4–1 deficit and tie the score 4–4. But Talbot gave up René Bourque's second and third goals of the night and Montreal stayed alive with a 7–4 win.

Therrien was pleased with the win but not with his team's loosey-goosey style. His message for Game 6 was direct—play a simple road game, don't take chances. He might as well have said: Don't take shots. Tokarski did his job. He made 31 saves and limited the Rangers to a single goal from journeyman Dominic Moore. But Lundqvist had an easy night as the Canadiens fired only 18 shots at him, and he stopped them all.

CHAPTER 4
STANDING OUT

No player in the Canadiens' recent history had as much impact on and off the ice as P.K. Subban. Everyone has an opinion about Subban, but, love him or hate him, you couldn't ignore him.

Subban was always the loudest voice in the room, the guy with the best fashion sense. He hung out with artists and entertainers. During the off-season, he might be spotted at the European soccer championships, in the pits at the French Grand Prix, or posing for a selfie with Novak Djokovic at Wimbledon.

He took nutritional advice from celebrity chef Antonio Park and was a regular patron at Park's eponymous Montreal restaurant where a two-ounce appetizer of genuine Kobe beef will set you back $98.

From the day he was drafted until the day he was traded for Shea Weber, Subban was always the center of attention.

A Good First Impression

Interviews at the NHL entry draft are usually predictable. The drafted player talks about how thrilled he is to be selected, how this is the greatest day of his career. He talks about how hard he worked to get to this point and how he knows that he will have to work even harder to earn a spot in the NHL.

General managers and scouting directors gush over the new additions and talk about how they never thought the player would be available when their selection came up.

As Canadiens general manager Marc Bergevin notes, it's part of the game.

"The only team that isn't surprised that their guy is available is the team that drafts first," said Bergevin.

But the Canadiens felt they had found a special player when they selected Subban in the second round of the 2007 draft. He was the club's third selection that year after defenseman Ryan McDonagh at No. 12 and Max Pacioretty at No. 22.

Forty-two players were selected before Subban's name was called, but the 18-year-old from the Belleville Bulls didn't sound like a second-round pick as he addressed the media in a small room in the basement of Nationwide Arena in Columbus.

"I'm going to make Mr. Gainey glad that he drafted me," Subban proclaimed. "I'm going to help this team win a Stanley Cup."

It was a bold statement, particularly coming from a second-round draft choice whose defensive skills were suspect. The scouting report on Subban described him as a high-risk, high-reward player, and he was a strange pick for a conservative team that stressed defense.

Subban then surprised reporters by noting that, even though he grew up in Toronto, the Canadiens had always been his favorite team.

That was because his father, Karl, immigrated to Canada from Jamaica and settled in Sudbury, a mining town in Northern Ontario. The community had a large French-Canadian population that followed Les Canadiens, and the elder Subban went with the flow. His allegiance remained steadfast even after he moved to Toronto to begin a successful career as a teacher and middle school principal.

"I remember visiting their house and being surprised to find Canadiens' memorabilia on the walls," said director of scouting Trevor Timmins.

As the media filed out of the interview room, the general consensus was that it was going to be fun covering P.K. Subban if he ever made it to the NHL.

A Good First Impression, Part Two

The Canadiens have never been known to rush a player's development. Since 1980, only two teenagers—Petr Svoboda and Alex Galchenyuk—have played in the NHL in the same year they were drafted.

As a second-round draft pick, it was predictable that P.K. Subban would serve an apprenticeship before getting a shot at the NHL. He spent two more seasons with the junior Belleville Bulls before making his professional debut with the Hamilton Bulldogs in 2009.

Subban was an instant hit in the American Hockey League. He scored 18 goals and added 35 assists in 77 games and had an impressive plus-46 rating. He was named to the AHL First All-Star team and the AHL All-Rookie team. Fans in Montreal were clamoring for a look at the youngster, and they received a sneak peek when he was called up for a pair of games against Philadelphia before the Olympic break in 2010. It was a tantalizing preview of things to come as he averaged more than 20 minutes of ice time and collected a pair of assists before returning to the minors.

But Subban's breakthrough came two months later in the NHL playoffs. Subban was concentrating on getting through the first round of the AHL playoffs when he was told to report to Bulldogs coach Guy Boucher's office following a Sunday night game in Hamilton.

P. K. Subban before the start of the NHL All-Star Skills Competition.
(Nick Wagner/Cal Sport Media via AP Images)

"I was told it was really important, and I asked myself: 'Am I in trouble?'" Subban recalled. "They said I wasn't, and [Boucher] told me I was being called up. He told me just to keep my game simple."

The Canadiens found themselves shorthanded because Jaroslav Spacek was sidelined by a virus. The call-up came too late for Subban to catch the last flight from Toronto to Montreal, but his father, Karl, gave him a 5:30 AM wake-up call Monday morning, and he arrived in time for the team's morning skate.

Many players take advantage of the time between the morning skate and the game to grab a nap, but Subban, who is a bundle of nervous energy at the best of times, said he was unable to relax before his playoff debut.

"I didn't expect to get called up at all," Subban said that night. "My focus less than 24 hours ago was to get out of the first [playoff] round and move on to the second [with the Bulldogs]."

If he was tired, it didn't show in his performance on the ice. Subban played a modest 10:02 in his team's 4–1 win over Washington in Game 6 of the Eastern Conference quarterfinal. He had two hits and a blocked shot and picked up an assist on the winning goal by Michael Cammalleri as the Canadiens evened the series at 3–3.

Subban was back in the Canadiens' lineup two nights later in Washington and helped the Canadiens eliminate the team that had finished the regular season with the best record in the NHL.

Subban hadn't been to Washington before his trip for Game 7, and he considered what awaited him in the nation's capital.

"Who knows?" he asked with a wide grin. "Maybe Obama will show up."

US President Barack Obama was not there for Game 7, but Vice-President Joe Biden was on hand to witness Subban's second NHL playoff game and what would become part of a series of disappointing playoff losses for the Capitals.

There wasn't an extra stall available in the cramped visitors' dressing room at the Verizon Center, and Subban had to make do with a folding chair in the middle of the room.

"I don't care where I dress; I'm just happy to be here," said Subban.

Subban was used sparingly in those first two games, but he was pressed into a larger role in the Eastern Conference semifinal against the Pittsburgh Penguins.

The Canadiens, who finished eighth in the Eastern Conference standings, were 10–1 underdogs against the Penguins, and their prospects looked even dimmer after the Penguins opened the series with a 6–3 win. The loss was compounded by an injury to Andrei Markov, the Canadiens' best defenseman. Matt Cooke collided with Markov, and the Russian veteran, who had a history of knee problems, had to be helped off the ice. He flew home to Montreal the following day, and the team announced that he would be out indefinitely with a lower-body injury. Markov missed the remainder of the playoffs with a knee injury that would require surgery and keep him on the sidelines for most of the next two seasons.

That opened the door for Subban. He was on the ice for 23:17 and picked up an assist as the Canadiens shocked the Penguins with a 3–1 win in Game 2. When the Canadiens deadlocked the series at 3–3 with a 4–3 win in Game 6, Subban led the Canadiens in ice time with 29:11.

The Canadiens beat the Penguins in seven games, but a red-hot Michael Leighton shut out Montreal three times as the Philadelphia Flyers won the Eastern Conference Final in five games.

The 2010 playoffs established Subban as an elite defenseman. He had a goal and seven assists in 14 games and averaged more than 20 minutes of ice time.

P.K. Deals with Racism

Racist comments proliferated on social media networks in the hours after Subban scored in double overtime to give the Canadiens a 4–3 win over the Boston Bruins in the opening game of the Eastern Conference semifinal series on May 1, 2014.

Fuelled by a string of playoff meetings, the Canadiens-Bruins rivalry was one of the fiercest in pro sport but, on this occasion, it took an ugly turn.

Unhappy Bruins fans tweeted comments like "That stupid n———r doesn't belong in hockey #whitesonly."

Influence Communications, a Montreal media monitoring and analysis company, determined that the N-word and Subban's name appeared in 17,000 tweets the day after the game, but it pointed out that the majority of them were not negative.

Some Boston fans, upset by suggestions that their city was a racist stronghold, expressed their disappointment with those issuing racist tweets.

"N———r was trending in Boston because P.K. Subban scored. It's a rare moment in my life to be ashamed to be a Bruins fan," read one tweet.

Another fan wrote: "I bet the Bruins fans calling P.K. Subban a n——r on Twitter have no idea his brother plays for their minor league team."

P.K. Subban's brother Malcolm Subban was drafted by the Boston Bruins in 2012 while the Boston roster included right winger Jarome Iginla, whose father is a black man from Nigeria and whose mother is a white American.

It didn't take long for the Bruins to distance themselves from the offensive slurs.

Team president Cam Neely issued the following statement the day after the game: "The racist, classless views expressed by an ignorant group of individuals following Thursday's game via digital media are in no way a reflection of anyone associated with the Bruins organization."

Several Boston Bruins players, as well as head coach Claude Julien, told CBC sports reporter Andie Bennett they condemned the offensive tweets.

"Those people are not our fans. They may think they are, but they are not," Julien said.

Boston mayor Marty Walsh also issued a statement.

"This is a disgrace," said Walsh. "These racist comments are not reflective of Boston and are not reflective of Bruins fans. I've said before that the best hockey in the world happens when the Bruins and Canadiens play each other, and there is no room for this kind of ignorance here."

Walsh said he and Montreal mayor Denis Coderre made a friendly wager on the series, and "we closed the conversation by wishing each other the best. I would hope that fans on both sides would follow this example."

Subban distanced himself from the controversy, saying that he had more important things to worry about than comments from ignorant fans.

This wasn't surprising because I had a long talk with Karl Subban in Minnesota earlier that season when he played hooky from his job as a middle school principal to join the Canadiens on their annual fathers' trip.

When the subject of racism came up he said: "Your potential lies inside of you; it gives you the ability to reach for something, to become something. So it doesn't matter what people say around you, it's not going to change what's inside of you. There's greatness inside of you."

As the momentum swung back and forth until the series reached a Game 7 showdown, Subban remained in the spotlight. There was a new controversy in Game 5 when Boston's Shawn Thornton sprayed Subban with a water bottle.

Subban played some good games, and in other games he was ordinary. There were questions about whether the controversy had thrown him off his game.

As coach Michel Therrien addressed the media before Game 7, he was asked about Subban, and his reply might have surprised people who liked to talk about the friction between the coach and his star defenseman.

"P.K. Subban has been phenomenal since the playoffs started, even to the end of the season," Therrien said. "He's a gamer, he's a guy who will bring his game to another level when the game will count. He's been a leader on the ice, definitely, for our club."

At the same time, Subban was preparing to play his role in the deciding game, a day after his 25th birthday. He had won the

Norris Trophy as the NHL's best defenseman the previous year, and he was no stranger to pressure situations. He was playing in the 10th NHL elimination game of his career, and it was the fourth time he was playing in a sudden-death Game 7.

The last time Subban faced elimination at the hands of the Bruins was on April 27, 2011, at TD Garden. The Canadiens lost in overtime after Subban had sent the game into extra time by scoring the equalizer with less than two minutes to play in regulation.

"Yeah, I wanted to do it again. I wanted to do it again the next shift," Subban said of his game-tying one-timer. "It was great to push it to overtime, but we didn't get the job done. I wanted to put another dagger in, but I didn't get my opportunity."

Subban said the 2011 loss provided him with incentive for the 2014 showdown.

"I'm sure I'll get my opportunity this time," he added optimistically of Game 7 in this series. "It's my job to make sure it counts.

"I remember losing [in 2011]. I thought that we had an opportunity to win. I remember going into overtime and them getting a bounce, a shot that bounces through a guy's leg, hits a leg, and goes in—that can be the difference in Game 7.

"This is going to be the biggest game of the year for us. For some guys, it's the biggest game of their career so far. It's fun. You've got to enjoy it. This is where legends are made.

"You have to enjoy it," Subban said of sudden-death in the playoffs. "I don't think I've played a game in this league nervous, and I'm not going to start to do that now."

Then Subban delivered the kind of boast that winds up on a bulletin board in the opponent's locker room.

"It's going to be great," Subban said of the game in Boston's TD Garden. "I can't wait for the crowd, the noise, the energy in the building. I can't wait to take that all away from them. I hope their crowd is louder than in here [at the Bell Centre]. I hope it gets nasty, I hope it gets dirty because at the end of the game when you're shaking hands, whoever wins, that's what the feeling's all about—it's knowing that you battled, you went through a war, and you know what? We're going to be at the end there standing tall."

The Canadiens backed Subban up by winning the deciding game 3–1.

"I thought we competed very hard, very hard against a bigger team, a stronger team, and a more experienced team," said Subban. "I think at some point a lot of people were saying 'don't poke the bear.' Well, I thought they gave us many reasons to keep competing throughout the series. At the end I'm just proud of my bunch—proud of the bunch of guys in this room. That's a character series win for us."

Subban said there was extra motivation in exorcising the demons from the Game 7 overtime loss in 2011.

"Anytime you're moving on to the conference finals it's a good feeling, but more importantly with the rivalry and against this team," said Subban. "Listen, it comes down to respect. I think we've done a lot of great things in this league since I've been here. Our team's done a lot, but we failed to get the respect that I think we deserve, and I think we earned that. I think more importantly, especially for the guys who have been here who were in that [playoff] run in 2010...and who were there the next year when we lost Game 7, we're just sick and tired of it. Sick and tired of, you know, people disrespecting us and not giving us the credit that we deserve. We're a good group of guys in here, we're a character group, and I think we earned a lot of respect today."

Unfortunately for Subban and the Canadiens, they were bounced by the New York Rangers in the Eastern Conference Finals. Any chance they had to win went out the window when Chris Kreider crashed into Carey Price in Game 1 and the goaltender suffered a sprained knee.

Dream Becomes a Nightmare

In the summer of 2014, Subban signed the richest contract in Canadiens history—an eight-year deal worth $72 million. He was 25 years old, and they thought he'd become one of the cornerstones of the team's future along with goaltender Carey Price and Max Pacioretty.

He made a major commitment to the community prior to the 2014–15 season, pledging to raise $10 million for the Montreal Children's Hospital. The Canadiens weren't particularly happy with this decision. While they couldn't publicly knock Subban for his generosity, there were some noses out of joint because they didn't learn about the donation until it was announced by the hospital. Some felt that Subban should have coordinated his giving with the team's charity, the Montreal Canadiens Children's Foundation.

He was arguably the most popular athlete in Montreal, and yet on February 19, 2015, Subban appeared to be begging for his job as he addressed reporters before a game against the Philadelphia Flyers.

There was widespread speculation that the Canadiens were thinking of trading Subban. After a promising start, the Canadiens had one of the worst records in the NHL. The loss of Carey Price early in the season doomed the team to mediocrity, but there was also a talk of a rift between Subban and his teammates.

"I think I'm part of the answer, not the problem," Subban told reporters after practice, adding that he wanted to remain a Canadien for the rest of his contract and for his career. "I told [former Canadiens GM] Bob Gainey when I was drafted I would do everything in my power to help the Habs win the Cup. That's never changed."

Coach Michel Therrien was also under fire, and there was a debate over whether he should be fired after a 3–2 loss in Colorado, a game that turned on a mistake Subban made in the third period. Therrien seemed to throw Subban under the bus with his postgame comments.

"The team worked hard. We deserved a better result," Therrien said. "It's too bad an individual mistake cost us the game late in the game.

"We believe that, as a coach, he [Subban] could have made a better decision at the blue line. He put himself in a tough position. We play as a team. When we don't, we could be in trouble, and this is what happened."

The comments added fuel to the long-held belief that Therrien didn't appreciate Subban's talents and reined him in by insisting that he concentrate on the defensive aspects of the game. Max Pacioretty contributed to the loss because he failed to get back after the puck went past Subban, and Therrien was criticized for singling out Subban while giving Pacioretty a pass.

As the Canadiens prepared to play the Flyers—a game the Canadiens would win 3–2 in a shootout—the captain accepted some of the blame.

Therrien also threw cold water on any speculation of a rift with his star player, saying he has a "very good relationship" with Subban.

"I would've said that about any player making that play at that time of the game," he explained. "We're very aware we have an exceptional athlete. We're happy to have him. It's our job to continue working with him."

Subban's rocky relationship with Therrien was a recurring theme during the four years they were together. In general, there was a belief that Therrien wasn't able to work with young players, a theory that doesn't hold much water when you look at his record in junior hockey, in the American Hockey League, and in Pittsburgh where he took the Penguins to the Stanley Cup Final with a team that included youngsters Sidney Crosby, Evgeni Malkin, Kris Letang, Jordan Staal, Tyler Kennedy, and Marc-André Fleury.

The idea that Therrien was picking on Subban took wings two years earlier when a weekly video shown on Habs TV designed to take fans behind the scenes showed Therrien berating Subban.

Fans were outraged by the coach's treatment of the young defenseman, but Subban laughed it off when I asked him if he was embarrassed by the video.

"He's trying to make me a better player," said Subban.

He went on to suggest that he was better prepared to accept the criticism than a teammate with a more fragile ego.

"I can take it, I'm not Lars Eller," he said.

Beginning of the End

The 2015–16 season was a disaster. It had started on a high note with a team-record nine consecutive wins, but the streak came to an end on October 27 in Vancouver.

Two nights later, the Canadiens lost to the Oilers 4–3, and goaltender Carey Price praised rookie Connor McDavid, who had collected two assists.

"He's a special player and the fans here are going to enjoy watching him play for a long time," said Price. He didn't mention that he had suffered a knee injury.

Price wasn't scheduled to play the following night in Calgary, and he watched rookie backup Mike Condon make 30 saves in a 6–2 win over the Flames.

When the Canadiens returned home, Price met with the team's medical staff, and the team announced that he had suffered a lower-body injury.

Condon, a Princeton grad with one season of pro experience, became the No. 1 goaltender. He posted a 5–2–2 record in Price's absence, but there was a sense of relief when Price returned on November 20.

Price beat the New York Islanders twice before facing the New York Rangers on November 25. He was cruising with a 3–1 lead when he made an awkward-looking save midway through the second period. He was slow getting up, but he continued playing. When the period ended, he told coach Michel Therrien that he couldn't continue.

"As a goaltender, you can tell when something is wrong," said Condon, who stopped 11 shots to wrap up a 5–1 win. "I was ready to go in."

The next day, Therrien said Price had aggravated the same lower-body injury, but there was no sense of panic. The Canadiens had the best record in the NHL at 17–4–2, and Price would be back in no time. At least, that's what everyone thought.

With each passing week, it became obvious that Price's injury was more serious than originally thought. He had suffered a sprained medial collateral ligament in his knee. The doctors determined he didn't need surgery, but the knee wasn't responding to treatment.

There was the occasional tease—Price was skating, he was taking shots, he's close to playing.

But the season ended with Price on the sidelines and the Canadiens fifth in the Atlantic Division and 13th in the Eastern Conference. Their 38–38–8 record left them 14 points shy of a playoff spot.

There was a dark cloud hanging over the team as the players cleaned out their lockers. Instead of accepting the fact that the Canadiens rely heavily on Price, the team was looking for a scapegoat and Subban was cast in the role.

If Price had stayed healthy, there wouldn't have been a crisis in the spring of 2016, but his absence led to Subban's departure.

When Subban was asked about his relationship with Pacioretty, he said: "We like each other, play together, respect each other, but, like, do I have to go over and make out to show my affection?"

Subban paused for a moment and then walked across the room and gave Pacioretty a bear hug, a show of affection that obviously embarrassed the captain.

Subban acknowledged that people may be put off by his personality.

"Sometimes I smile, and people tell me to wipe that stupid smile off my face. Doesn't mean I have to stop smiling," said Subban. "Just because Andrei Markov isn't laughing and smiling doesn't mean that he's not pulling pranks in the dressing room. That's why I laugh. The perception that people can create [about me] isn't real."

Responding to the relationship between Subban and Therrien, General Manager Marc Bergevin said it's not the job of a coach to be loved by all of his players.

"It's to be respected, and sometimes it's called tough love," the GM said. "Across the board, every team I've been on [during his NHL playing days], it was the same thing. So I'm not saying P.K. does like or doesn't like Mike. I know one thing—since Mike's been here, P.K. has won one Norris Trophy, has been nominated for another one, leads our team in ice time. Overall, under Michel Therrien, P.K. has progressed to a really young, fine defenseman."

The Trade

As the hockey world gathered in Buffalo for the 2016 NHL entry draft, there was renewed speculation that the Canadiens were shopping P.K. Subban.

General Manager Marc Bergevin brought a temporary halt to the talk when he met the media on the afternoon prior to the draft.

"I have no intention of trading P.K. Subban," declared Bergevin. "He's an important part of our team."

When he wasn't traded during the draft, the assumption was that he would remain with the Canadiens, but a deal to move the most popular Canadien was already in the works.

Nashville general manager David Poile broached the subject before the first round of the draft on Friday afternoon, and the talks continued through the weekend. Both sides played their cards close to the vest, and the announcement that Subban had been traded for Shea Weber came as a shock. The news broke on June 29, two days before a no-trade clause in Subban's contract was scheduled to kick in.

Bergevin characterized the deal as a "hockey trade" with the Canadiens giving up some age—Weber is nearly four years older than Subban—and puck-moving skill in return for the more physical and more defensive-minded Weber.

But it was difficult for fans and the media not to speculate on whether Subban was sent packing because of the friction with his teammates and coach Michel Therrien. Reports noted that none of his teammates were on hand when he made his pledge to the Montreal Children's Hospital and that Subban was a no-show at a team Christmas party and other player-organized events. And when it came time to nominate a player for the NHL Foundation Player Award, which recognizes community service, Subban was ignored, despite his much-publicized pledge of $10 million to the hospital. The nod went to Pacioretty, whose foundation was partnered with the Montreal General Hospital and the Montreal Canadiens Children's Foundation.

Bergevin said reports of Subban not fitting in were blown out of proportion because of "the market we're in."

"We always look to make a story where there isn't any," he said. "Yes, P.K.'s different—we're not going to hide that—but there was never an issue, never a problem. I fought with my teammates in practice; it happens all the time, so I think it was blown out of proportion."

When Bergevin was asked whether the Canadiens' camp would be quieter without Subban, he acknowledged that Subban and Weber have different personalities.

"But I don't want to take anything away from P.K. because he's made the way he is and he's a good person and he's got a lot of qualities," he said.

Subban was on vacation in France when he learned of the trade and was devastated by the news.

"Listen, while I was a Montreal Canadien, there's nothing but fantastic times for me," Subban said. "I have to say that out of all the fan bases in the National Hockey League, the Montreal Canadiens' fans and community and the province of Quebec have probably embraced me more than any other player has felt in any other city. It's give-and-take. I've done a lot of things in that community, and they've supported me since the day that I was drafted. So I've always felt wanted by the fans and the community there.

"On the business side of things, the Montreal Canadiens paid me a lot of money two years ago to do what I do for a living," said Subban. "At the end of the day I just wanted to come in and do my job. But obviously right now I'm going to a team that wants me, and the Montreal Canadiens felt that they had to take it down a different path."

While Subban generally took the high road after the trade and reaffirmed his commitment to the children's hospital, he delivered more than a few broadsides at his former employers when he hosted the final gala at the annual Just for Laughs Comedy Festival. The August 1 gig at Montreal's Place des Arts was booked before the trade as a means of raising funds for Subban's foundation, and it became the hottest ticket in town after he was sent packing.

Subban came on stage dressed in a three-piece pink suit and had the audience laughing from the start.

"I went to Europe this summer, and while I was there I did all the things a normal Canadian would do: I drank good wine, I hung out at beautiful beaches, and got traded for Shea Weber."

Subban talked about his newfound love for country music and dedicated a couple of songs to his former teammates and managers.

"There's this great song by Zach Paxson that I'd like to send out to all my former teammates trying to bring the Stanley Cup back to Montreal by playing under Michel Therrien's system. You know what that's called: 'Good Luck with That!'"

Subban also had a dedication for General Manager Marc Bergevin.

"Just to show there's no hard feelings, I gifted him this great song called 'Take This Job and Shove It,'" said Subban.

"I know what you're all thinking; I'm just as surprised as you are," Subban told the audience. "Right off the bat, let me just say that I also can't believe this happened. I mean obviously I'd heard the rumors, but like most of you, I thought they were just that, rumors. I mean it's Montreal, right? So when my agent actually called me and said, 'P.K., I just want to let you know you've been ... booked to host a Just for Laughs gala,' I couldn't believe it. I was fired up, I was floored."

At one point, Subban took an indirect swipe at owner Geoff Molson, whose family began brewing beer back in the 18th century.

"I'm thirsty, can someone get me a beer?" asked Subban. "Get me a good one, none of that Molson crap."

Subban also had some fun with his new home south of the border.

"If there's one thing I've tried to do in all the cities I've played in, it's immerse myself in the local culture. In Belleville, I learned how to sail. When I moved to Montreal, I learned how to speak French—right ladies? And in Hamilton, I learned how to breathe through my mouth," he joked, as the audience laughed. "So now that I'm living in Nashville, it's time I learned more about..." he said, pausing before he delivered the punchline: "That's right, getting pulled over by the cops."

Ticket sales for the event and special P.K. Subban Just for Laughs jerseys raised $130,000 for the hospital.

Just for Laughs chief operating officer Bruce Hills explained how plans for the event began. "I approached him and said let's do something, raise money for his foundation for the children. He said yes, and it's been a blast ever since."

"It's just another way for us to raise money for children and for a good cause," said Subban.

Subban, who visited the hospital on a weekly basis while living in Montreal, said he will do what he can to keep the connection he has made with many patients.

"It's up to my team and the hospital to make them feel comfortable about it and to understand that I'm not leaving. I'm leaving to play hockey, but I'm not leaving them," he said.

Subban may have been traded to Nashville by the Canadiens, but he said Montreal will always have a place in his heart.

Subban said he always knew being traded was a possibility, no matter what Bergevin said to the contrary.

"I knew there was a lot of chatter leading up to the draft and free agency. I thought that where there's smoke, there's fire," said Subban. "Nobody ever told me I would be traded, but when you see the rumors and you start getting messages from reporters and all this stuff you figure that something's going on."

Let's Go, Preds

When the 2017 Stanley Cup playoffs began, there were many fans in Montreal hoping to see a final matchup between the Canadiens and the Nashville Predators.

When the Canadiens lost to the New York Rangers in the first round, Subban and the Nashville Predators became the focal point for fans' interest.

Paulo Branco, the owner of the popular bar Chez Serge, was among the many Montrealers who were heartbroken when Subban was traded to Nashville in summer 2017 and he was also devastated when his beloved Habs fell to the Rangers.

That's when he came up with the idea of at least temporarily changing the name of his bar to Chez Subban.

"I wouldn't have changed the bar's name if the Canadiens were still in the playoffs," Branco told Christopher Curtis of the *Montreal Gazette*. "I bleed red, white, and blue. I'm still, first and foremost, a Canadiens fan.... P.K. was a person who always really impressed me. I'd crossed paths with him a few times over the years, and he was just such a kind, classy person.

"I've been in the bar business going on 22 years, and I've come across a lot of hockey players in my establishments. The only other player who had as much class as P.K. was [former Canadien] Mark Streit."

Branco recalled a time he saw Subban interacting with children at a restaurant in Westmount.

"There must have been 15 kids ... I think it was someone's birthday, the kids were going crazy. And P.K. took the time to speak to all of them. It must have been 25 minutes of his day, and he spoke to them like they were adults. He respected them—he didn't just tap them on the head and move on."

Branco called on a graphic artist friend to design a new sign for his bar, and the establishment quickly became a must-go destination for Subban fans. The bar became so popular on nights when the Predators were playing that Branco had to remove the city's only mechanical bull.

News of the name change reached Subban when he was in St. Louis for Game 2 of the Western Conference semifinals. Subban reportedly had a huge smile on his face when NHL.com reporter Arpon Basu showed him a picture of his new namesake.

"I'll have to stop by for lunch when I get there next summer," Subban said.

"He'll be well received when he comes here, I can tell you that," Branco said. "And, if he wants, maybe he can take the Stanley Cup here with him. We'll drink some Molson Canadian right out of the cup."

That drink will have to wait. When the Predators lost to Pittsburgh in the Stanley Cup Final, the mechanical bull returned and Chez Subban reverted to Chez Serge.

CHAPTER 5
IT'S ONLY MONEY

Locking Up Price

Expect the unexpected.

That is Marc Bergevin's catchphrase, and he delivered it on July 2, 2017.

The free-agency frenzy had been quiet in Montreal. Bergevin had made a big splash in mid-June when he acquired home-grown forward Jonathan Drouin from the Tampa Bay Lightning. Drouin's career in Tampa had been marked by fits and starts, but Bergevin saw the 22-year-old as part of the answer to the team's struggling offense. He did the unexpected when he sent defense prospect Mikhail Sergachev to Tampa Bay in return.

Bergevin had always resisted dealing what he called his assets—players he had identified as core players, high picks in future drafts,

Carey Price makes a save against the Devils. *(Graham Hughes/The Canadian Press via AP)*

or top prospects like Sergachev, who had been drafted ninth overall in 2016. A Russian who played junior hockey with the Windsor Spitfires, Sergachev was an imposing physical specimen. But Bergevin, who constantly preached that you can never have too many defensemen, felt Sergachev was the price he had to pay.

As the free agent market opened on July 1, Bergevin signed free agent Karl Alzner to shore up the left side of the defense and added some spare parts.

Normally, the general manager addresses the media at the end of the day, but shortly before Alzner spoke to the media gathered around a speakerphone at the Canadiens' practice facility in suburban Brossard, the team announced that Bergevin would postpone his remarks for a day.

The announcement touched off a wave of speculation. The day had ended without deals for unrestricted free agents Andrei Markov and Alex Radulov. Bergevin had a little more than $10 million in cap space after signing Drouin to a six-year, $33-milion deal and giving Alzner $24 million over five years. The question was whether Bergevin had enough money to satisfy both Russians.

As the media gathered for a second day in Brossard, Bergevin stunned them with the announcement that goaltender Carey Price had signed an eight-year extension worth $84 million—a cap hit of $10.5 million a season. He had one season remaining on a six-year deal with a cap hit of $6.5 million.

Bergevin had listed the Price deal as one of his priorities. He didn't want the franchise goaltender going into the final year of his contract with the possibility of becoming an unrestricted free agent in 2018. But the length and the size of the contract were both surprising.

At 29, Price was at the top of his game. He had an Olympic gold medal and a World Cup title. He won the Vezina Trophy as the NHL's top goaltender and the Hart Trophy as the league's most valuable player. And goaltending coach Stéphane Waite said he had the potential to get even better. Waite pointed to Price's strong work ethic and his desire to be best.

He would be 38 at the end of the new contract, which kicked in with the 2018–19 season. But the bigger concern over the length of the deal was not Price's age but his history of knee injuries, including a strained ligament, which sidelined him for most of the 2015–16 season.

Bergevin said the team did its due diligence.

"In hockey, there's always the possibility of injuries, but our medical people checked him out and we're not concerned," said Bergevin.

As for the money, Price had a pretty good idea of what he wanted and he got it. The Canadiens had set the table for the goaltender two years earlier when they gave defenseman P.K. Subban an eight-year deal worth $9 million a season.

With the new deal, Price became the highest-paid goaltender in NHL history as well as the highest-paid Canadien of all time. While there's no doubt he has been the key to any success the Canadiens have enjoyed in recent years, the contract does pose some problems for Bergevin going forward. He has committed nearly a quarter of his cap space to Price and defenseman Shea Weber.

"Giving one player a big amount makes things a little more difficult," admitted Bergevin. "But that's part of my job to manage that. In an ideal world, we would have given him less. But that's just part of the negotiation process."

Price made it clear that he wasn't interested in giving the Canadiens a hometown discount. He also dismissed any suggestion that he wanted to play closer to his roots in Western Canada.

"I never thought about playing anywhere else," Price said from his summer home in Kelowna, British Columbia. "It's a great place for me. I never thought about putting on another uniform. I just thought it would be too weird, I guess.

"There's no better place to play hockey. I'm honored to be able to wear a Canadiens uniform for the rest of my career. This is all I've ever known, and it's all I ever will know, I hope."

"It was five years ago when we extended Carey Price; now, five years later, we're going to make sure he finishes as a Montreal Canadien," said Bergevin. "We have, in my opinion, one of the best [goalies] in the business, if not the best. We want to keep him and make sure he's here for the rest of his career."

Price said he feels right at home in Montreal.

"It's hard at times, but other times the most fun you're going to have in the entire NHL is playing well in Montreal," he said. "There's nothing that compares to it."

Building a competitive team and winning a Stanley Cup with a goalie as the team's highest paid player will be no easy feat, but Bergevin says it's possible.

In the 2017–18 season, there were only three other teams that featured a goaltender as the highest-paid player. They were the New York Rangers with Henrik Lundqvist ($8.5 million), the Columbus Blue Jackets with Sergei Bobrovsky ($7.425 million), and the expansion Vegas Golden Knights with Marc-André Fleury ($5.75 million).

Full Disclosure

Some of the greatest players in NHL history were grossly underpaid. For many years, salaries were a dark secret.

Gordie Howe accepted whatever the Red Wings offered him because management told him he was the team's highest-paid player. Years later, he learned there were seasons when that honor actually belonged to fellow Hall of Famer Ted Lindsay.

Canadiens legend Maurice Richard never made more than $50,000 in a season. In his final season, 1959–60, he was paid $25,000, and his total career compensation was less than the current NHL minimum of $650,000.

One of the problems was that the Original Six teams had a tight control on the labor market. When the NHL Players Association was formed in 1967, minimum salary levels were established, but the explosion of salaries began with two incidents in the early 1970s.

The first was a blockbuster story by longtime colleague Red Fisher in the defunct *Montreal Star*. Fisher managed to obtain a list of all the player salaries in the NHL.

The league was quick to describe the list as inaccurate, but it became required reading for the players. They were just as quick to recognize that the numbers were correct, and they began asking questions about why they weren't making the same as some players with comparable skills and production.

A year later, the NHL got competition from the World Hockey Association, which began playing then. The Philadelphia Blazers lured colorful Derek Sanderson away from the Boston Bruins with a $2.6-million deal that made him the highest-paid professional sports athlete. Bobby Hull topped that when he signed with the Winnipeg Jets for $2.75 million, earning him the nickname the Golden Jet.

Sixty-seven players, including Canadiens J.C. Tremblay, Réjean Houle, and Marc Tardif, would jump to the new league, and NHL teams were forced to raise their salaries to retain players.

While some teams, including the Canadiens, are still reluctant to reveal salary details when they announce a signing, that information is readily available on a number of websites. Agents use these numbers when they negotiate contracts, and they regularly employ outside help to determine comparables.

From the player's point of view, there is one downside to the public dissemination of salaries. Big-money contracts carry with them the expectation of big-money performances. Nobody knows this better than defenseman Patrice Brisebois, who was a rookie when the Canadiens won the Stanley Cup in 1993. He earned a modest $93,564.

A decade later, Brisebois hit the jackpot. The Canadiens paid him $4 million, which made him the highest-paid player in team history. It also made him the No. 1 target for the boo birds when something went wrong.

Brisebois was an offensive defenseman, and he had difficulty winning one-on-one battles. And sometimes on the power play a puck got by him at the point, giving the defending team a short-handed opportunity.

Montreal Gazette columnist Jack Todd led the detractors, giving the defenseman the nickname Patrice Breeze-by.

The razzing became so bad that General Manager Bob Gainey was compelled to come to Brisebois' defense after an exhibition game against Buffalo on September 28, 2003.

In the middle of the second period, fans began booing Brisebois each time he touched the puck. After scoring in the third period to put the cap on a 3–1 victory, Brisebois turned to the crowd and motioned with his hand for them to turn up the volume.

When the game was over, Gainey made a rare appearance at the postgame news conference and blasted the fans.

"We don't need those people, we don't want those people, they're jealous people, yellow people," Gainey said of the fans who booed Brisebois. "I think they're a bunch of gutless bastards, to be honest."

"Our message to them is to stay away," added Gainey. "We don't need you."

Brisebois said he was happy someone was finally sticking up for him.

"I appreciate his support," he said. "I've always said there are people who like me and appreciate me. I play for them, and my friends and family."

Brisebois moved to the Colorado Avalanche in 2005 after the Canadiens declined to pick up an option on his contract that would have paid him $4.5 million. After two years in the Rockies, Gainey brought him back to Montreal in 2007. During his second stint in Montreal, Brisebois had a reduced role, but he was looked on as a savvy veteran who was passing his experience on to youngsters like Mike Komisarek, Ryan O'Byrne, and Josh Gorges.

He also was seen as a guy whose production exceeded the expectations that came with his salary. He was paid $700,000, and everyone agreed he earned every penny of it. Nobody begrudged him when he received a $50,000 raise the following season.

CHAPTER 6
PLAYING WITH PAIN

Max Pacioretty got off to a slow start in the 2016–17 season. After 26 games, he had scored seven goals and added 11 assists, and he had moved up and down the lineup.

On numerous occasions, he was asked if he was hurt. At first, he would address the issue by saying that injuries were a part of the game and that there wasn't a single player in the dressing room who was 100 percent healthy. Pacioretty knew about real pain. On March 8, 2011, Boston's Zdeno Chara ran him into a stanchion at the Bell Centre, and his season ended with a concussion and a broken vertebra. Whatever was bothering him was a minor irritation by comparison, and he began to greet repeated questioning by rolling his eyes and ignoring the query.

Shortly before Christmas, Sportsnet reporter Eric Engels revealed that Pacioretty had been playing with a hairline facture in his foot. Engels noted that the injury had healed, and it wasn't long before Pacioretty picked up the scoring pace. He finished the season as the team's leading scorer with 35 goals and 67 points.

Hockey is a contact sport, and it takes its toll over an 82-game season. Players and teams are reluctant to provide information on injuries, other than to describe an ailment as lower-body or upper-body. One of my favorite examples of sketchy information revolved around an injury to forward Martin Rucinsky on December 18, 2000. He left the game against the Columbus Blue Jackets after taking a big hit on his first shift. During his postgame news conference, Coach Alain Vigneault said Rucinsky suffered an upper-body injury, but it didn't appear to be serious.

Two days later, the Canadiens announced that Rucinsky had undergone successful knee surgery.

Putting Savard Back Together

My father-in-law was an ear, nose, and throat doctor who said that doctors were akin to tradesmen. Cardiologists, he would say, were electricians; internal medicine specialists were plumbers; and orthopedic surgeons were carpenters.

The last description was apt when it came to the work Dr. Ted Percy performed to put Serge Savard's leg back together after it was shattered in a collision with a goal post in a game against the New York Rangers on March 11, 1970.

"The nets were anchored in those days, and there were a lot of players who were injured when they went into the posts because they didn't move," said Savard. "I remember the incident well. I lost an edge, and I knew I was going into the post, and there was nothing I could do to avoid it. I was in a lot of pain, and I knew it was broken."

Broken doesn't adequately describe the injury. The leg was shattered in several places. Savard was taken to hospital where the leg was set, but, a day later, it was obvious that Savard needed more than a plaster cast.

"I didn't see Dr. Percy that first night. He didn't become involved until the next day," recalled Savard. "When I got up, I could feel the bone moving inside the cast, and when Dr. Percy examined it, there were numerous breaks and some bone chips. He needed to put the leg back together with screws and a plate. I was only 24 at the time, and I didn't know whether I would ever play again."

Savard returned to action the following season, but he suffered another setback in a January 30, 1971, game against the Toronto Maple Leafs. Bobby Baun caught Savard with a hip check, propelling him into the boards. The screws were dislodged and Savard had another date with Percy in the operating room.

"This time, he did a bone graft, taking some bone from my hip and using it to repair the leg," said Savard.

The second operation left Savard on the sidelines for almost a year, and he was surprised when former teammate and close friend John Ferguson asked him if he was interested in joining Team Canada for the historic Summit Series against the Soviet Union in the fall of 1972. After retiring from the Canadiens, Ferguson had joined the Team Canada staff as an assistant coach, and he thought Savard's mobility would be an asset against the skilled Soviet team.

"I was surprised because I missed almost two full seasons with my leg," said Savard. "I had changed my style because I wasn't as fast as I was when I broke into the league. I was more of a defensive player, but Fergy felt I could help the team."

The series almost ended prematurely for Savard. In a practice prior to Game 4 in Vancouver, a Red Berenson shot caught Savard on the ankle, and he suffered a hairline fracture. Savard was fortunate that that there was a break between Game 4 and the resumption of the eight-game series in Moscow.

While Team Canada headed to Europe for a pair of exhibition games in Sweden, Savard returned to Montreal for treatment and expressed his determination to rejoin the team for the games in the Soviet Union. Savard was able to get 10 days of rest at home before traveling to Europe. He did so despite the objections of the Canadiens' management and his doctors. Savard sat out the two exhibition games in Sweden as well as Game 5 in Russia, but dressed and played in the final three games of the series.

"I was lucky it was just a crack and not another fracture," said Savard. Team Canada did not lose any of the five games in which Savard played, winning four and tying one.

Savard said Percy allowed him to continue a Hall of Fame career that spanned 16 seasons, 14 of them as a Canadien.

"There is a reason why I called him Brother André. He performed miracles," said Savard.

The members of Team Canada were presented with commemorative watches after their victory, and Savard decided to present his to the man who made his participation possible.

"When I arrived back in Montreal, the very first time I ran into Dr. Percy I gave him the watch and told him that he deserved it because I would never have recovered in time to play in the series if it wasn't for him."

Dr. Percy wore that watch constantly until his death in 2017.

Savard paid another tribute to Percy in 2016. An active horseman, Savard paid $110,000 for a promising filly at the 2016 Ontario yearling sales, and he named the horse Percy Bluechip.

The horse lived up to her name when she made her debut as a 2-year-old in a stakes race at Ontario's Georgian Downs on July 9, 2017. The filly set a Canadian record for a 5/8-mile track, pacing the mile in 1:51²/₅.

A Pain in the Neck

Whenever a player has to be taken off the ice on a backboard, there's reason for concern. That was the case on November 20, 1999, when Brian Savage suffered a neck injury in a game against the Los Angeles Lakers at the Staples Center.

Here's the way Red Fisher described the incident in the *Montreal Gazette*:

> The injury was a strange one, almost self-inflicted.
>
> Savage, playing on his 12th shift of the game, had jumped on the puck, carried it to the Los Angeles blue line. Then, head down, he lashed his stick at the puck—and whiffed the shot. However, the force of his swing carried him into an onrushing Ian Laperriere, sending Savage to the ice, legs kicking, arms waving. Scary.
>
> The damage to the bottom of his neck was done when his head snapped downward at the moment of impact.
>
> He lay on the ice for several minutes before anxious medical people called for a stretcher to remove him from the ice, whereupon he was immediately taken to the hospital for a series of tests.

As the Canadiens returned to their hotel that night, the mood was somber, but there was reason to be optimistic.

"The first thing you think of is paralysis," said defenseman Eric Weinrich. "Luckily, he's moving his legs and hands and arms. I'm not worrying about how it affects the team. You just worry about, you know, the person."

When the players went to bed on Saturday, all they knew was that the prognosis on Savage was squeaky clean, that tests at the hospital failed to reveal problems. Not to worry, they were told.

The MRI results later told a different story. The players were gathered in the hotel lobby the next morning when they learned the extent of their teammate's injuries.

When Jeff Hackett asked if everything was okay, he was told that Savage had suffered a fracture in one vertebra, with a strong suspicion of a second break. There was also swelling on his spine that indicated damage to the ligaments between the vertebrae.

"The first thing you've got to do is pray for him. It's very scary," said Hackett. "Obviously, you've got to worry about the person, not the hockey player."

"I just got the news," said Shayne Corson. "It's sad. When you see him laying on the ice, hockey becomes very secondary. You think about his life. You think about his wife and the child they're expecting. You tell yourself that the only thing that matters is for Brian to run around, play with his kids, get healthy, getting back to the team. You think about him doing the things normal people do. What's more important than playing with your kid, doing all the things fathers do with their first-born?"

"I was shocked, obviously," said Scott Thornton. "The word we got in the dressing room was that he had a little bit of a burner, which is muscular, you know, or whatever. This must be a pretty serious injury.

"When it happened, I didn't think it was that bad," said Thornton. "I mean, he was still moving his legs and whatnot, you know. I thought he was okay. At worst I thought he might have had a concussion. That's something I've never seen in hockey.

"During the game, we didn't know what was going on," added Thornton. "After the game, we were told he's going to have some tests done, but we think it's just a burner and this and that. We were sort of relieved after the game. To wake up this morning with that kind of news is devastating."

The news wouldn't get better over the next few days. Tests revealed a break in a second vertebra. After three days in a Los Angeles hospital, Savage was allowed to fly home. He arrived at the Montreal airport wearing a collar to stabilize his neck, and he immediately went to the Montreal General Hospital where team physician David Mulder discovered more damage. The number of broken vertebrae rose to three. Dr. Mulder said the injury had been life threatening, and his prognosis was that Savage's season was over and that he might have to consider another line of work.

But Savage, who took a circuitous route to the NHL, was determined to play again and underwent a rigorous rehabilitation. He was back on the ice in mid-February and was cleared to play two weeks later.

It was a toss-up who was more nervous when the Canadiens met the Atlanta Thrashers on March 2, 2000—Savage or his wife, Debbie.

"I'd say we were both pretty nervous," Debbie said as she watched her husband play for the first time since his accident. "He tried not to show it, but I can read him pretty well, and he was nervous."

"No, she was far worse than me," said Savage. "I was nervous, but I think she worried. I didn't tell her I was coming back until Sunday."

Savage said he dreamed about scoring a key goal in his return, but he settled for a night when, by his own admission: "I didn't do anything spectacular."

But he played his first game for the Canadiens since the Laperriere collision. He received medical clearance to return to game action a week earlier after missing 44 games. The accident brought an abrupt end to a strong start to the season. Savage, whose early-season heroics earned him the not-necessarily-flattering nickname Mr. October, scored 12 goals in his first 20 games.

Brian Savage gets ready to play against the Atlanta Thrashers on Monday,
March 6, 2000, following 44-game absence due to a fractured vertebrae.
(AP PHOTO/Paul Chiasson)

"I felt good, but it's tough when you haven't practiced with the team, when you've just been skating alone. There's a big difference between Sergei Zholtok's passes and passes from Gates [trainer Gaetan Lefebvre]."

Savage saw limited action on a line with Zholtok and Oleg Petrov. He played 13 shifts totalling a little more than 10 minutes, won his only faceoff, had two first-period shots, and was credited with a hit.

"I had some contact out there, and it felt okay," he said. "The toughest part was in the second period when there were some penalties and I sat for about 15 or 20 minutes. I was tight when I got out there and my legs felt heavy."

The contact was the one thing that had Debbie Savage worried.

"I kept seeing the neck brace he had to wear after the accident," said Debbie. "It looks like he's playing okay out there, but I'm still a bit afraid every time he goes into the corner and there's some contact.

"It might have been better if I saw a practice," said Debbie, who was eight months pregnant with the couple's first child. "I saw the open practice they had a few weeks ago, but there was no hitting or anything."

Savage said the highlight came on his second shift when his picture was flashed on the scoreboard and the crowd acknowledged his return.

"That felt really good. I was nervous when the game started, very anxious, but it was a good kind of nervous. The crowd helped me feel comfortable."

Savage played a dozen seasons in the NHL, including parts of eight seasons in Montreal. It was a good run for a player who stepped away from the game as a teenager in Sudbury, Ontario. Savage was an all-around athlete; in addition to hockey, he competed in track and golf. He was one of the top junior golfers in Canada and felt that if he played major junior hockey, there wouldn't be enough time to work on his short game. Savage's father was a teacher, and he felt the travel demands of junior hockey would have a negative impact on his son's grades.

Savage had a relatively normal high school career at Lo-Ellen Secondary School. He ran track, played golf, and helped the school qualify for the provincial high school hockey championships. While high school hockey in Ontario is low-key, Savage drew the attention of some college scouts. After sifting through scholarship offers for golf and hockey, he accepted a hockey scholarship at Miami University in Ohio.

Under today's draft system, Savage would have gone through college as an undrafted player because the draft is limited to seven rounds. But the draft went nine rounds in 1991 when Savage was wrapping up a freshman year in which he had five goals and six assists in 28 games. Savage was selected in the eighth round, No. 171 overall.

It was a gamble that paid off for the Canadiens. In his final season at Miami, Savage had 37 goals and 21 assists in 38 games. He was invited to join Canada's national team for the 1993–94 season and was part of the last amateur team to represent Canada at the Winter Olympics. Savage earned a silver medal at Lillehammer where Canada lost to Sweden in a shootout for the gold.

CHAPTER 7
WHEELING AND DEALING

Irreconcilable Differences

There was no chance for a long-term reconciliation between goaltender Patrick Roy and the Montreal Canadiens.

Roy made that clear at a news conference in the Laval Sheraton hotel on December 4, 1995, two days after he told team president Ronald Corey that he was through. But the mercurial goaltender didn't shed any more light on the events that led to his suspension and the Canadiens' decision to trade him.

"I was humiliated," Roy said repeatedly. He was referring to the Saturday night game at the Forum where the Detroit Red Wings beat the Canadiens 11–1. Coach Mario Tremblay didn't pull Roy from the game until he had allowed nine goals in less than 30 minutes. Roy exchanged angry words with Tremblay as he went to the bench, then engaged in a staring match with the coach before turning to Corey and saying, "I've played my last game for the Canadiens."

"I didn't apologize because it would not have made any difference in the long term," Roy said when asked about a Sunday meeting with General Manager Réjean Houle. "It might have made a difference, but not in the long term. The same problems would have come up again."

When pressed, Roy refused to elaborate on the nature of his problems, but his agent, Robert Sauvé, made it clear that his difficulties with Tremblay existed before Saturday night's game.

"Mario said in the papers this morning that there were problems, but it came to a head Saturday night," Sauvé said. "Patrick was humiliated, he was frustrated, and it all came out. I think there was bound to be conflict because Patrick and Mario are the same type of person. They are both roosters."

Patrick Roy gestures to the crowd after being jeered when he made a save on a routine shot during the team's 11–1 drubbing at the hands of the Detroit Red Wings on Saturday, December 2, 1995. *(AP Photo/Montreal La Presse-Bernard Brault)*

The Canadiens said they would continue to pay Roy, who earned $4 million as part of a four-year, $16-million deal, until he was traded, but that he would have no contact with the team. While his former teammates were making their annual Christmas visit to sick children at Sainte Justine Hospital, Roy was next door presenting a $500,000 check for the construction of the Patrick Roy wing at Ronald McDonald House, which provides accommodation for the parents of seriously ill children.

The check represented a personal contribution of $100,000, with the remainder coming from the fund-raising efforts of the player's foundation.

Roy didn't waste any time making the presentation, and ducked reporters and cameramen. He made himself available at the news conference later, but he wasn't any more forthcoming about the incidents that led to what he called his separation from the Canadiens.

Roy did apologize to Montreal fans for a gesture he made during the game. The fans sarcastically cheered Roy when he made a save after the Wings went ahead 7–1, and he responded by throwing his arms in the air as if he had won his third Stanley Cup.

"It was a mistake, a big mistake, and I'm very sorry," Roy said. He went on to thank the Montreal fans and the media. He also called the Canadiens a classy organization and offered thanks to Corey and former coach Jacques Demers who had been replaced by Tremblay earlier in the season. He didn't thank Tremblay or Houle.

"When I heard the news [of their hiring], I wanted to take a cold shower," said Roy, repeating what he said at the time of the hiring on October 21. But he quickly added that he had no reason to believe they couldn't do the job. Tremblay and Houle became coach and general manager, replacing Demers and Serge Savard. There were more than 100 reporters, photographers, and cameramen at the Laval gathering. There were 20 TV cameras, more than double the number required to cover a Saturday night game at the Forum. Most of Montreal's TV stations carried at least a portion of the news conference live during their 6:00 PM newscasts.

The turnout provided a counterpoint to a much smaller gathering earlier in the day at the Forum, where Corey gave reporters his view of the controversy. Corey said no player is bigger than the team and that he stands 100 percent behind Tremblay and Houle.

When asked whether there had been any attempt to resolve the dispute, he merely said that both sides agreed Sunday that there was no way to settle the conflict.

Signs of Roy's popularity extended well beyond Laval. The windows outside the Forum boutique were crammed with Roy posters, game sweaters, loose-leaf binders, and even a Patrick Roy jigsaw puzzle. When it comes to marketing the team, Roy held a special place.

While Roy said he was ready to move on and that he had many years left in the NHL, he also noted that the matter was out of his hands as he awaited a trade.

"I hope it's done quickly," said Roy. "In the meantime, it's up to me to stay in shape and be ready."

Sauvé said he had asked Houle for two considerations.

"I asked that it be done as quickly as possible, and I asked that he try to find a competitive team."

Sauvé smiled when asked whether Roy would welcome a trade to the Colorado Avalanche, the former Quebec Nordiques.

Avalanche general manager Pierre Lacroix used to be Sauvé's boss, and he was Roy's agent when he signed his $16-million deal in 1993.

There was a report out of Denver that the Avalanche had offered goaltender Stéphane Fiset and forward Mike Ricci in return for Roy, but when the deal was done a few days later, it was backup goaltender Jocelyn Thibault who came to Montreal along with forwards Andrei (The Russian Tank) Kovalenko and Martin Rucinsky. Canadiens captain Mike Keane joined Roy on the flight to Colorado.

The Canadiens insisted on Thibault because he was younger that Fiset and they believed that he had more potential. He would spend the better part of three seasons as the No. 1 goaltender in Montreal before he was traded to Chicago for Jeff Hackett in 1998.

Language played a large part in the decision to throw Keane into the mix. A classic rink rat, the hard-working Keane was a natural leader who was popular with his teammates, and he was elected to serve as the Canadiens' 23rd captain prior to the season.

But Keane found himself in the middle of a controversy when Mathias Brunet of *La Presse* asked him if he intended to learn French.

"Why learn French?" Keane replied. "I'm not a spokesman. I just liaise between players and management. Everyone here speaks English. I don't feel the need to speak French."

It was the wrong answer. Brunet's article created a backlash among nationalists in Quebec. The province was in the middle of a referendum campaign to determine whether it would separate from Canada, and French-English tensions were high. Bernard Landry, a cabinet minister who would later become premier of

Quebec, took the Canadiens' management to task, saying it had a responsibility to ensure that its employees learn French. Trading Keane to Colorado and replacing him with the French-speaking Pierre Turgeon rid the Canadiens of a headache.

While trading one of the best goaltenders in NHL history put the Roy deal on the top of the list of worst trades made by the Canadiens, General Manager Serge Savard toyed with the idea of trading Roy before the 1995–96 season. While Savard wouldn't confirm any of the deals he discussed, he did talk with Colorado, and Roy's name came up.

"As a general manager, you're always thinking of ways to improve your team," Savard said. "I didn't go out with the idea I was going to trade Patrick Roy, but I was willing to listen to what teams had to offer. I would have made a deal but not the deal they ended up making, and I wouldn't have traded Mike Keane."

Colorado was interested in Roy because Lacroix had been the goaltender's agent. After adding Vladimir Malakhov, Pierre Turgeon, and Mark Recchi, Savard was interested in Owen Nolan.

Savard said he also had his doubts about head coach Jacques Demers. After winning the Stanley Cup in 1993, the Canadiens lost in the first round to Boston the following season and then missed the playoffs in the lockout-abbreviated 1994–95 season. They opened the 1995–96 season with four consecutive losses, but it was the way they lost that concerned Savard. The Canadiens appeared uninterested and were outscored 20–4.

"I thought Jacques had lost the room," Savard said in an interview for this book. "It happens with coaches. We saw it with Pat Burns who then had the same problem when he was in Toronto and Boston."

Before Savard could trade Roy or fire Demers, he found himself out of work when Corey cleaned house. He fired Savard and Demers and brought in the inexperienced Houle as general manager. At the time, the former two-way forward was doing public relations work for Molson Brewery.

Corey's unhappiness with the way the team was going was aggravated by the impending move to a new building the following March. He had 3,000 more tickets to sell, and it wasn't going to be easy if the team was losing.

"Obviously, I was disappointed," said Savard. "I talked to Mr. Corey before the season started, and I told him I thought we had a Stanley Cup team, that we were just missing one or two players. It was sad to see what happened. The '93 team that won the Cup was a young team, but they got rid of all the leaders—Guy Carbonneau, Lyle Odelein, Mike Keane—guys with character."

The Rise of Halak

The best-selling T-shirt in Montreal in the spring of 2010 featured the outline of a stop sign with the word "Halak" in the middle.

A local entrepreneur created the unauthorized apparel as an homage to Canadiens backup goaltender Jaroslav Halak, who had earned the admiration of Montreal fans with a strong performance late in the season and a playoff run that ended with a loss to the Philadelphia Flyers in the Eastern Conference Final.

Carey Price, who was the fifth overall pick in the 2005 draft, started the season as the No. 1 goaltender for the Canadiens, but he struggled. It was the only time in his NHL career, prior to the

2017–18 season, that he would finish with a losing record, and, by mid-January, Halak had been promoted to the top spot.

Halak, who backstopped Slovakia to a surprising fourth-place finish at the Olympic Games in Vancouver, would start 24 of the final 34 games, posting a 14–6–4 record. Price was 2–4–2 in his 10 starts.

"It [the Olympics] gave me a chance to prove I could play on the big stage," Halak said. "I'm happy with the way my season turned out. I improved my mental aspect and got more experience. This year, if I allowed a bad goal or played a bad game, I was able to put it aside."

Coach Jacques Martin had an easy decision to make when he had to select a starting goaltender for the postseason. Halak started 18 of the 19 playoff games after getting the Canadiens off to a good start with a 3–2 overtime win in Washington. He faltered in Game 3, and that opened the door to Price to make his only start. It proved to be a disaster as Price allowed four goals on 36 shots, and Martin went back to Halak, who led the Canadiens back from a 3–1 deficit in the best-of-seven series.

The Slovak persevered in seven games against Washington and slipped by Sidney Crosby and the Pittsburgh Penguins in another seven-game series. Halak was the toast of Montreal, and the T-shirts were flying off the shelves.

But the hopes for a 25th Stanley Cup ended in the Eastern Conference Final, and Halak would have had to be perfect to change the result because Flyers' goaltender Michael Leighton had the series of his life. Leighton posted three shutouts as Philadelphia won the series in five games.

The fun began as the Canadiens cleaned out their lockers. Halak and Price were both scheduled to become restricted free agents on July 1. Halak said he hoped General Manager Pierre Gauthier could find room for both of them, but that prospect appeared unlikely. Price was at the end of an entry-level contract, which paid him $850,000, while Halak was making $800,000. Both were in line for a raise. Gauthier had about $11 million in cap space but had only 14 players under contract. The situation was compounded by the fact that Halak was eligible for arbitration and he was represented by Allan Walsh, an aggressive agent who would certainly argue that Halak's performance merited a salary in the $4–5 million range.

Montreal fans were divided in their loyalties, and several polls indicated that they favored Halak over Price. The playoff run was one reason for that, but they were also rooting for the underdog and there were few bigger underdogs than Halak. While Price has that first-round pedigree from 2005, Halak was drafted in the ninth-round two years earlier at No. 271 overall. Halak wouldn't have been drafted at all in today's NHL with the draft now limited to seven rounds.

He moved from the Bratislava junior team in Slovakia to the Maineiacs of the Quebec Major Junior League where he was coached by Clement Jodoin, who had previously served as an assistant coach with the Canadiens.

On June 17, the Canadiens traded Halak to St. Louis for prospects Lars Eller and Ian Schultz.

But the deal didn't end the debate. Here's how my colleague Red Fisher viewed the deal:

What you do, if you're Canadiens GM Pierre Gauthier, is trade the guy who got them there in what now must stand as the mother of all brain-dead decisions in recent memory. What was this guy thinking of?

Where was Gauthier on those nights when Jaroslav Halak was winning regular-season and playoff games with more than 40 shots to handle? Downtown Minsk? Where was Gauthier on the night Halak wasn't beaten until Washington's 52nd shot in another astonishing winning performance?

I don't know when the Canadiens' GM thought about this trade, but I do know he couldn't have had his thinking cap on when he made it. He can talk all he wants about something called a salary cap and the difficulty of fitting Halak into it. What Gauthier is really saying is that it's a fit for Carey Price, who has yet to demonstrate he belongs in the NHL, but not for Halak, who was one of the truly great achievers in the playoffs.

What awaits Canadiens fans, you ask? Fit to be tied, that's what.

Fisher didn't get things wrong too often, but, in retrospect, Gauthier made the right choice. Price bounced back the following season when he led the NHL with 38 wins. In 2015, he swept the Hart Trophy as the league's most valuable player and the Vezina Trophy as the top goaltender. While Canadiens fans are still waiting for Price to lead them to the Stanley Cup, he struck gold at the 2014 Olympic Games in Sochi and the 2016 World Cup.

Halak has had a decent career—he's in the top 15 among active goaltenders in wins and goals against average—but he has been plagued by injuries. He finished the 2016–17 season in the American Hockey League, but that said more about the dysfunctional New York Islanders front office than Halak's performance.

Subsequent events also proved there was no way the Canadiens could have held on to both goaltenders.

After a long summer of negotiations, Price agreed to a two-year bridge deal on September 3, 2010, and on July 2, 2012, he signed a six-year deal with a cap hit of $6.5 million. In 2017, he received an eight-year extension that will make him the highest-paid goaltender in history with a $10.5-million cap hit beginning with the 2018–19 season.

As for Halak, the Blues gave him a four-year deal averaging $3.75 million a season, and he went into the 2017–18 season with one more year on his four-year deal with the Islanders, which has a $4.5-million cap hit.

Jaro Thanks the Fans

Two months after he was traded, Halak made a return visit to Montreal to thank the fans. He appeared at a sporting goods store in a suburban mall to greet fans and sign autographs in return for donations to a children's hospital.

"I love Montreal, and I wanted a chance to thank the fans for all their support in the years I was here and to do something good for the community," said Halak, who stopped in Montreal to take care of personal matters before reporting to the Blues. He was in his native Slovakia when the Canadiens announced they had traded him on June 17.

An estimated 5,000 fans formed a line that snaked through the lower level of the mall the day Halak visited. They carried sweaters, goalie pads, gloves, sticks, and other memorabilia to be autographed by Halak, who became a folk hero when he led the Canadiens to the Eastern Conference Final. Fans were asked to donate $20 for each item signed, with the proceeds going to the hospital.

"That was the charity Jaro chose, and we're happy to say we raised more than $22,000," said David Schatia, the Montreal lawyer who represented Halak.

The only disappointment was that Halak wasn't able to accommodate all the fans who showed up, even though the goaltender—who earned a reputation for busy nights between the pipes—worked overtime. The session was scheduled to run from 2:00 to 4:00 PM, and it was close to 6:00 PM—an hour after the mall's normal Saturday closing time—when security personnel shut things down.

Halak moved into the concourse to address the thousands of fans who were still on hand, and then addressed a smaller group that had been unable to enter the building.

"His people in the States said we could expect 500–600 people, and I thought we'd get 2,000–3,000," said Dino Digiannantonio, one of the store's owners. "The first people showed up at 8:00 AM, and the line just kept getting bigger."

Price Makes His Debut

The decision to trade Halak wasn't the first time the goaltender was snubbed in favor of Price.

Halak was the No. 3 goaltender in the American Hockey League with the Hamilton Bulldogs in 2006–07 with a 2.17 goals against average. When Cristobal Huet suffered a left hamstring injury in mid-February, the Canadiens recalled Halak from the Hamilton Bulldogs, and he leapfrogged over backup David Aebischer.

Halak posted a 10–6–0 record with a .906 save percentage, but it wasn't enough to lift the Canadiens into a playoff spot. Montreal finished two points behind the eighth-place New York Islanders, and Halak prepared to rejoin the Bulldogs for the American Hockey League playoffs.

But General Manager Bob Gainey had a different idea. Price, who was the Canadiens' first-round draft in 2005, suddenly became available after his junior team, the Tri-City Americans, lost to the Seattle Thunderbirds in the first round of the Western Hockey League playoffs.

Price ended his junior career on a less-than-stellar note. He gave up seven goals as Seattle defeated the Tri-City Americans 7–2 to win the best-of-seven series in six games.

Gainey thought the playoffs provided a perfect opportunity to assess the 19-year-old Price at the pro level. Price joined the Bulldogs for the final two games of the regular season, and, after he posted a 1–1 record with a 1.53 goals against average and a .949 save percentage, Gainey decided the youngster was ready for another challenge.

The problem was how to break the news to Halak without hurting his feelings. Gainey solved that problem when he announced the Canadiens were allowing Halak the opportunity to play for his native Slovakia in the IIHF world championships in Moscow.

But the biggest loser in the decision to start Price in the play-offs was Yann Danis, who had been demoted to Hamilton after serving as José Theodore's backup in the 2005–06 season. Danis had shared the goaltending job with Halak and finished the season with more wins than the Slovak. His career took another backward step with the arrival of Price.

Hamilton coach Don Lever had his marching orders—Price was No. 1. Price lived up to the billing. His only hiccup was in Game 1 of the Western Conference Final against the Chicago Wolves. Price struggled and was replaced by Danis with the Wolves holding a 4–2 lead midway through the second period.

"He got a little overwhelmed in that game," said Lever.

It turned out okay when Danis stopped 17 of the 18 shots he faced and defenseman Dan Jancevski scored in the second overtime to give Hamilton a 6–5 win.

That was the only action Danis saw in the series. Two nights later, Price was back in goal, and he stopped 22 shots as the Bulldogs edged the Wolves 3–2.

Price finished the playoffs with a 15–6 record, a 2.06 goals against average, and a .936 save percentage. The Bulldogs clinched the Calder Cup with a 2–1 win over the Hershey Bears at Hamilton's Copps Coliseum, and Price was presented with the Jack Butterfield Trophy as the playoff MVP.

Deadline Day

The speculation starts shortly after the new year as teams begin to assess their positions, and it builds until deadline day—the last day for teams to make trades before the playoffs.

The strangest deadline deal I can recall occurred on March 23, 1999, when the Canadiens traded captain Vincent Damphousse to the San Jose Sharks for three draft picks.

There had been a lot of speculation that Damphousse would be moved because he was eligible to be an unrestricted free agent on July 1 and the Canadiens felt he was on the downside of his career. He had only 12 goals in 65 games and General Manger Réjean Houle signalled that the struggling Canadiens were headed for a major rebuild two weeks earlier when he traded leading scorer Mark Recchi.

But as the Canadiens boarded their chartered aircraft for a flight to Edmonton on deadline day, it appeared that Damphousse was staying in Montreal.

Two hours into the flight, with the clock ticking closer to the 3:00 PM deadline, the Canadiens made a stunning announcement— Damphousse, who was sitting in the rear of the plane, had been traded.

Donald Beauchamp, the team's director of public relations, conferred with Damphousse and then huddled with the media who were sitting behind the coaches and team management at the front of the plane. Beauchamp said Damphousse asked for some time to process the news. He asked the media to respect the player's privacy and said Damphousse would be available after the plane landed in Edmonton.

The media gathered in the terminal and watched as the players filed off the plane.

A few players offered quick reactions to the deal, but there was no sign of Damphousse.

After 20 minutes, it was obvious that Damphousse wasn't getting off the plane because the aircraft began backing out of the gate. It took off with Damphousse aboard for the return flight to Montreal so that he could join the Sharks in Toronto.

The only member of the media who wasn't upset was Pierre Rinfret, the play-by-play announcer for the French-language broadcasts on radio station CKAC. Rinfret had used a trip to the plane lavatory as an excuse to stop by Damphousse's seat long enough to record what turned out to be an exclusive interview.

Houle took a lot of heat for the timing of the trade, but he insisted that the deal only came together after the plane took off from Montreal.

Recchi Sets an Example

Damphousse might have stolen a page from Recchi's playbook when he refused to meet the press.

The Canadiens were in St. Louis on March 10 when Recchi was traded to Philadelphia for Dainius Zubrus. He had been the subject of trade rumors for several weeks, and he probably knew there was a deal in the works because he wasn't available after an afternoon practice.

Shortly after 5:00 PM, the Canadiens announced the trade, and reporters staked out the lobby of the Adam's Mark Hotel, hoping to catch Recchi on his way to the airport.

But Recchi showed the same elusive moves that had served him well on the ice. He boarded a service elevator and slipped out of the hotel through a loading dock.

Recchi didn't get away scot-free, though. RDS reporter Luc Gélinas and cameraman Paul Buisson jumped into their rented van and headed to the airport. They caught Recchi checking in for his flight to Philadelphia and had the only reaction from Recchi from Montreal.

"Big Paul knew we would have time because he was used to checking his equipment, and he knew that Recchi would need time to check his equipment and his sticks," said Gélinas. "He was surprised to see us, but he agreed to talk."

Recchi also recorded some comments for a fan line maintained by the Flyers and said he was happy to be returning to Philadelphia, where he had many friends. He also reflected on the irony of joining John LeClair and Eric Desjardins, two players who went to Philadelphia in the 1995 trade that brought Recchi to Montreal.

"They're good players who have blossomed into superstars," said Recchi.

While the trades weren't unexpected, the mood in the Canadiens' camp was subdued if only because the deals were a tacit admission that the Canadiens were going to miss the playoffs.

Saku Koivu looked as if he had lost his best friend. And that, Koivu said, is exactly what happened when the Canadiens traded Recchi.

"He was my linemate, but he was also a very close friend," an emotional Koivu said the morning after the trade. "I think we all expected something to happen, but it was still a shock when I heard the news. I didn't have a very good night."

Koivu said he talked to Recchi before he left for Philadelphia, and the veteran winger had mixed feelings.

"He was relieved that it was over and he was going back to Philadelphia, but he was also disappointed because he wanted to stay in Montreal," Koivu said. "But hockey is a business, and these things happen."

Coach Alain Vigneault said the trade reflected the financial side of life in the National Hockey League.

"This wasn't a hockey decision; it was an economic decision," Vigneault said. "There's no doubt that Mark Recchi has been the best hockey player on this team over the past three or four seasons. He's a guy who comes to play every night. He plays with emotion and he's a leader, but we weren't going to be able to keep him and we made the best deal we could."

The Canadiens felt they had to deal Recchi because, like Damphousse, he was eligible to become an unrestricted free agent on July 1, and the team didn't feel it could re-sign him.

Defenseman Stéphane Quintal was also headed to free agency that season and attempts to trade him at the deadline fell through. On July 1, Quintal signed as a free agent with the New York Rangers and was only too happy to share his views on the move—and some very good wine—with the media.

A week after he signed a four-year, $11.4-million contract, he invited some reporters to Buonanotte, an Italian restaurant known for its wine list and high-powered clientele. The Canadiens had offered Quintal $10 million over four seasons but said his decision to leave was about more than money. He was reluctant to go into details, but it was obvious that he was unhappy over the departure of his good friend, Vinnie Damphousse.

The general feeling was that New York would be a perfect fit for the urbane Quintal, but it didn't work out that way. Quintal struggled in the 1999–2000 season, and, when the Rangers placed him on waivers, he was claimed by the Blackhawks. After one season in Chicago, Quintal was back home in Montreal. The Canadiens reacquired him for a fourth-round draft choice, and he played his three final NHL seasons in Montreal with a contract he signed in New York.

Take Off Your Uniform

Getting traded on a plane en route to a game is something different, but Michael Cammalleri is one of the only players to ever be traded in the middle of a game.

It happened on January 12, 2012, when the Canadiens were playing the Boston Bruins at TD Garden. A few minutes into the third period, someone in the press box noticed that Cammalleri wasn't on the bench.

"Did you see Cammalleri get hurt?" he asked.

"No," came a reply.

A few minutes later, there was a report that Cammalleri was being held out because he was being traded, but the Canadiens public relations staff said it was unaware of any deal.

When I arrived in the dressing room after the game, I learned that Cammalleri had been told to take a cab back to the Ritz-Carlton, the hotel the team checked out of earlier in the day. We had to wait another half hour before General Manager Pierre Gauthier revealed that Cammalleri was going to Calgary as part of a deal involving multiple players and draft picks.

There was a holdup because the key player coming to Montreal was winger René Bourque. The announcement was delayed until after the Calgary-Anaheim game that night because Bourque was serving a five-game suspension for elbowing Washington's Nicklas Backstrom in the head. By delaying the deal until after the trade, Bourque had to miss only one game with his new club.

The timing of the trade was curious because, two days earlier, Cammalleri appeared to throw his teammates under the bus, although the bilingual nature of the Montreal market led to some confusion.

Arpon Basu of NHL.com and François Gagnon from the French-language *La Presse* newspaper were talking to Cammalleri after practice, and the player vented his frustration over a season that would end with the Canadiens dead last in the Eastern Conference.

The problem arose after the TSN television network quoted Cammalleri's comments. The words, which were spoken in English, were translated into French by Gagnon, and, when TSN brought them back to English, this is the way it looked: "I can't accept that we will display a losing attitude as we're doing this year. We prepare for our games like losers. We play like losers. So it's no wonder why we lose."

In Basu's story, Cammalleri didn't use the word loser, but he did suggest that the Canadiens had slipped into a losing mentality.

A day later, Cammalleri made an attempt at damage control when he spoke to his teammates before the morning skate and the game against the Bruins.

"That's really none of your business," he said curtly when asked about his message to his teammates. "[Wednesday] was a little bit crazy. It's an emotional game—we're sitting in 12th spot. It's not fun to lose, you always want to do more. That's all."

"I made some comments after my interview yesterday that I thought were pretty [politically correct] with regards to the competitive advantage a winning team has in their mentality, and the lack thereof of a losing team," added Cammalleri. "I didn't think it was groundbreaking news. It was some pretty impressive journalism to make all that out of that."

It wasn't the first time that Cammalleri had expressed his unhappiness that season. Cammalleri found his ice time cut after Randy Cunneyworth replaced head coach Jacques Martin in mid-December. In December, he questioned the coach's approach toward the power play after the Canadiens went 0-for-5 in a 4–0 loss in Winnipeg.

"Our power play has been struggling [and] I think we have to change things up, get a little more creative," Cammalleri said. "I think it's a copout to say we have to get more shots, more bodies to the net. I think we have to move bodies around and look for shots from different spots."

Cammalleri, who was on pace for the least-productive season of his career, said chemistry has been elusive.

"We're definitely not clicking on the chemistry. Sometimes you find with your linemates that you're finding each other, and we're struggling with that now," said Cammalleri. "I think we're walking a fine line between keeping it simple and hard and not creating any hockey plays."

He didn't come right out and say it, but mostly Cammalleri was arguing for more Michael Cammalleri on the power play.

Gauthier insisted that the loser comments had no bearing on the decision to trade Cammalleri.

"I didn't have any problem with what he said because it showed emotion," said Gauthier. "I'd rather see emotion than people who didn't care. I just spoke with Mr. Cammalleri, and he understands what's happening, and I explained to him what's happening with the team. He never asked to be traded. He's part of the team and he cares a lot, and that's why he made those comments."

Gauthier said the trade had been in the works for a while.

"This is a trade that [evolved from] other talks we've had since about December 1," he said. "It's very difficult to make deals because of the salary cap, but we've been trying for all those weeks to get bigger."

The Canadiens did that, subbing the 6-foot-2 Bourque for the 5-foot-9 Cammalleri.

"We have a lot of young players who have joined the club like [defenseman Raphael] Diaz who aren't very big, and we felt it was important to get bigger up front," Gauthier said. "We need to score harder goals, not the fancy ones, not the outside shots. The outside shots don't go in anymore. That's why Mr. Bourque was very attractive to us, because he scores most of his goals in those hard areas."

There was an interesting footnote to the trade. When Cammalleri was told he was being traded, he asked if he could keep his No. 13 jersey, and Gauthier told him he could—if he paid $1,250.

Gauthier and the Canadiens took some heat for refusing Cammalleri's request, and, a few weeks after Gauthier was relieved of his duties on March 29, team owner Geoff Molson sent the sweater to Cammalleri.

"Just received a handwritten letter from Geoff Molson and my jersey from last game as a Hab," Cammalleri tweeted. "Much appreciated thank you. Merci."

The Smurf Brigade

While deadline day is a chance to tweak a roster is preparation for the playoffs or to dump a player before he reaches free agency, the heavy lifting is done in the off-season when the draft and free agency allow teams to make major changes.

The Canadiens had that opportunity in 2009 when General Manager Bob Gainey decided it was time to part with captain Saku Koivu. The Finn had been the face of the Canadiens for most of his 13 seasons in Montreal. He became a symbol of courage as he played through knee and eye injuries and a season-long battle with cancer. But the injuries had taken their toll and Gainey wanted to bring in some fresh faces. Koivu had also become a distraction because he stubbornly refused to learn French.

There was an expectation that Gainey would use the opportunity to add some size to the roster, but the moves he made around free agency resulted in a smaller lineup.

The makeover began on June 30 when the Canadiens acquired Scott Gomez from the New York Rangers. Montreal sent Chris Higgins, Pavel Valentenko, Ryan McDonagh, and Doug Janik to New York for Gomez, Tom Pyatt, and Michael Busto in a deal that haunts the Canadiens to this day.

It should have been a straight-up two-player deal involving Gomez and Higgins with each team ridding itself of a problem.

Gomez won the Calder Trophy as the rookie of the year with the New Jersey Devils in 2000, and the Rangers signed him to a seven-year deal worth $51.5 million in 2007. Gomez's production went down after moving across the river to Manhattan, and the Rangers were anxious to move his contract.

Higgins, a New York native, had been a first-round draft choice in 2002. He had 72 goals in his first three NHL seasons, but his production tailed off in season 4 and there were concerns that the former Yale star was enjoying the nightlife in Montreal a tad too much.

The Rangers wound up as the big winner in the trade because the Canadiens threw in McDonagh, who was a sophomore at the University of Wisconsin.

Montreal selected McDonagh as the 12th overall pick in the 2007 draft, which also produced Max Pacioretty at No. 22 and P.K. Subban at No. 43. As the story goes, Gainey soured on McDonagh after he went to watch the defenseman play at Wisconsin and caught him on an off night. He was traded despite the protestations of chief scout Trevor Timmins.

McDonagh would emerge as the best player in the deal. He left Wisconsin after his junior year, and, after half a season in the AHL, he was promoted to the Rangers. He became the team's top defenseman and was elected captain in 2014.

Gainey said Gomez was the key to his rebuilding program. He said the acquisition sent a message to free agents that the Canadiens were ready to make a run for the Cup. Michael Cammalleri signed as a free agent early in the day on July 1, and Gainey said the Los Angeles Kings scorer was excited over the prospect of playing on Gomez's wing. As the media was gathering for a 9:00 PM press conference with Gainey, the club announced that Brian Gionta, who had enjoyed some outstanding years as Gomez's linemate in New Jersey, had signed.

While all three possessed skill, the one thing that was obvious was that the Canadiens were smaller. Gomez was 5 foot 11; Cammalleri was 5 foot 9; and Gionta was 5 foot 7.

Cammalleri and Gionta signed five-year contracts with the Canadiens as free agents, while Gomez had five years remaining on the deal he signed with the Rangers. Gionta was the only member of the trio to remain in Montreal for the duration of his contract.

Cammalleri had difficulties accepting a reduced role under coach Randy Cunneyworth and was sent packing.

Gomez's decline in New York continued in Montreal. In his first season with the Canadiens, he collected 59 points and was the team's second-leading scorer behind Tomas Plekanec. In his second season, he had 38 points and had become a defensive liability with a plus-minus rating of minus-15. A knee injury limited him to 38 games in the 2011–12 season, and he scored two goals and added nine assists.

On February 5, 2011, Gomez scored the Canadiens' only goal in a 4–1 loss to the New Jersey Devils. The goal would be Gomez's last for more than a year. Gomez played in 60 of the Canadiens' next 90 games—he missed 30 of those games due to injury—and he failed to score in the final 29 games of the 2010–11 season, a seven-game playoff series against the Boston Bruins, and the first 24 games he played in during the 2011–12 season. Gomez had 122 shots on goal without scoring. The drought ended on

February 9, 2012, when he scored on a power play to help the Canadiens to a 4–2 victory on Long Island.

"He's been a real leader, and he's stayed positive through all the talk about not scoring," said Max Pacioretty, who scored his first NHL hat trick that night. "It was nice to see him get the monkey off his back."

"It's nice to score; it's been a long time," Gomez said. "The most important thing is that we got two points. We have to win every game. It's taken us too long to learn how to win, and now we have to keep it going. Scoring goals is good, but you play games to win."

The Canadiens didn't win enough games that year, and Gomez's position with the team was tenuous going into the 2012–13 lockout. Marc Bergevin replaced Pierre Gauthier as the general manager, and he planned to open some cap space by burying Gomez and his $7.357 million cap hit in the American Hockey League.

Bergevin ran into a problem when the new collective bargaining agreement required teams to count any AHL player's salary in excess of $900,000 against the cap. The CBA did allow teams to buy out two contracts in the 2013 or 2014 off-season without counting the cost of the buyouts against the cap.

The only proviso was the team couldn't buy out injured players. To avoid any risk of a hockey-related injury, the Canadiens told Gomez to go home when he reported to training camp on January 13, 2013.

The NHL Players Association wasn't happy that Gomez was going to sit until he could be bought out the following season. They argued that, while Gomez was being paid, it would be difficult for him to stay in shape if he wasn't playing. The agreement was revised to allow each team to use one of its buyouts prior to the abbreviated 2013 season. With the revised agreement in place, Gomez was placed on unconditional waivers and became a free agent on January 17.

"Guys come and go—it's part of the business," one teammate noted. "But Gomer will be missed because he was a great teammate and whenever we went out, he picked up the tab."

CHAPTER 8
SOME RUSSIAN TALES

If You Want Loyalty, Get a Dog

General Manager Marc Bergevin faced a dilemma following the 2016–17 season. He wanted to retain two potential unrestricted free agents—veteran defenseman Andrei Markov and right winger Alexander Radulov.

The expectation from the fans and the media was that Bergevin's task would be easy. Markov had played his entire 16-season NHL career in Montreal and he felt a comfort level in the city. Signing him had never been a problem, and his cap hit—$5.75 million—hadn't changed in 10 seasons.

Radulov had played only one season in Montreal, but it was a pivotal year in his career. He wore out his welcome in Nashville

April 22, 2017: Andrei Markov hustles after the puck during Game 6 against the Rangers at Madison Square Garden. *(Kostas Lymperopoulos/Cal Sport Media via AP Images)*

when he broke curfew during the 2010 playoffs, and he returned to the KHL.

In the spring of 2016, he expressed a desire to finish his career in the NHL. He was second in the all-time KHL scoring list behind Sergei Mozyakin, but there were questions about his character.

Character has always been a concern for Bergevin, but he has also shown a willingness to gamble. A year earlier, he signed Alexander Semin, a Russian whose NHL career had been in decline. Semin was out of shape when he showed up at training camp and played only 15 games before he was released and moved to the KHL. It was written off, no-harm, no-foul, management thought, because Semin signed for a mere $1.1 million.

It was going to take more cash to sign Radulov, and Bergevin did his due diligence. He talked to newly acquired defenseman Shea Weber who had played with Radulov in Nashville. He talked to former teammate Sergei Fedorov who was the general manager of CSKA Moscow, Radulov's team in the KHL. The reports coming back were positive. All agreed that Radulov was a talented, hard worker whose maturity was once an issue.

As he approached his 30th birthday, Radulov was married and embracing fatherhood for the first time. Bergevin gave him $5.75 million on a one-year deal.

Radulov lived up to expectations. He worked hard and filled a hole on right wing and on the power play. He played at both ends of the ice and helped Russian-American Alex Galchenyuk cope with a second-half slump.

Radulov professed his love for Montreal, its passionate fans, and his teammates. Nobody was too concerned when there was no announcement of a contract extension during the season because everyone assumed that Bergevin wanted to wait so that he wouldn't have to protect Radulov leading up to the Las Vegas expansion draft. Radulov denied a report that he was seeking a seven-year deal.

The expansion draft came and went and so did the opening day of free agency, and there was no news concerning Markov or Radulov. There were reports Markov was holding out for a two-year deal worth $6 million a season and that Radulov's asking price was $7 million a season over six years. Bergevin refused to comment on either report prior to the NHL entry draft, but he did say: "We have our limits."

Bergevin addressed the media on July 2, and he had mixed news. On the positive side, he announced that goaltender Carey Price had agreed to an eight-year extension worth $84 million. The deal, which kicks in with the 2018–19 season, made Price the highest-paid goaltender in NHL history.

The news on Markov and Radulov was less encouraging. Bergevin said he had made his final offer to the Russians, and he also noted that he had cap space to sign only one of them.

"It's first come, first served," said Bergevin.

When a reporter asked whether Radulov should express his loyalty after Bergevin took a chance on him, the general manager reflected on the reality of pro sports when he said: "If you want loyalty, get a dog."

On July 3, the Dallas Stars signed Radulov to a five-year contract with a cap hit of $6.25 million. The Stars enlisted Jamie Benn to help sell the deal, and the Dallas captain envisioned Radulov on a line with himself and Tyler Seguin.

There's some confusion over where the Canadiens were in the Radulov talks. Radulov said the Canadiens made one last-ditch attempt to keep him. They offered to match the Stars' offer, but Radulov told them he had already committed to Dallas.

Bergrevin insists that he made the same offer before Radulov accepted the Dallas offer. This might have been a face-saving move, but there's also a theory that the Canadiens were wary because Radulov and his wife were divorced by midseason and there was concern that a single Radulov might get out of control.

The Markov situation dragged on through the summer, and the two sides were unable to reach a deal.

Markov eased off on his request for a two-year contract, but he had grown accustomed to that $5.75 million even though his expiring three-year deal was front-loaded and he was only paid $4.25 million for the 2016–17 season. Bergevin's final offer was $4 million plus the potential to earn another $1 million in bonuses.

On July 25, the Canadiens signalled they were going in a different direction when they signed 39-year-old Mark Streit to a one-year deal worth $700,000. Streit wasn't going to fill the top-four spot vacated by Markov, but he was seen as a valuable addition to the power play.

Two days later, Markov announced that he would not return to the Canadiens. In a sometimes emotional conference call, Markov expressed regret that he was unable to reach a deal with the Canadiens.

He said he didn't consider offers from other NHL teams because it would be too difficult for his family—he got married earlier in the month and has five-year-old twin boys from an earlier marriage—to adjust to a new North American city. He said he would play in the KHL—he later signed with Ak Bars Kazan—and hoped to represent Russia in the 2018 Winter Olympics in South Korea. With the NHL opting to skip the 2018 Games, Russia won the gold medal but Markov was not selected for the team.

The irony is that the Canadiens could have met Markov's price if they had been willing to throw in the money they paid Streit. The veteran Swiss defender played only two games with the Canadiens before he was placed on waivers and assigned to the Laval Rocket. He balked at joining the AHL team and both sides agreed to terminate his contract.

The Quiet One

I have a theory about predicting the future success of Russian players in the NHL. I believe their success is tied to their willingness to learn English.

The theory dates back to 1989 when Igor Larionov and Vladimir Krutov joined the Vancouver Canucks. They were two-thirds of the famed KLM line along with Sergei Makarov, but Larionov and Krutov couldn't have been more different from each other in their approach to the NHL.

Larionov was a North American the day he arrived in Vancouver. He spoke English. He was familiar with the popular TV shows and the latest Hollywood movies. He went on to have a Hall of Fame career that included three Stanley Cup wins in Detroit, and today he's a highly respected agent and wine merchant.

Krutov couldn't speak English and showed little interest in learning. He was out of shape when he arrived in training camp. He was an old-school Soviet who viewed the regular season as an opportunity to work his way into shape for the world championships. He lasted only one year before returning to Europe and died of liver disease at the age of 52.

"Larionov was a very urbane, worldly educated sort of guy and was excellent in English, while Krutov, not so much," former Canucks general manager Pat Quinn said after Krutov's death. "He didn't have any English and was a peasant in terms of his upbringing. He was certainly a good hockey player, but, unlike Larionov who was able to make the transition quite easily and welcomed it, Krutov was homesick right away.

"It was a terrible experience for him. He really wasn't enjoying it all, and he didn't want to be here. You could see flashes of his hockey ability from time to time but not enough. He couldn't sustain it. He wasn't conditioned well. His passing is sad. We never got to know him really well."

The same can be said of Andrei Markov. He played 16 seasons in Montreal but offered only rare glimpses into his private life. He was in his fifth season in Montreal before anyone heard him speak English. Prior to that, reporters relied on teammate Oleg Petrov or Russian journalists to serve as translators.

"He doesn't say much in Russian," noted one journalist. "He's pretty shy."

When Markov did begin to feel comfortable speaking English, he wasn't prepared to share even the most mundane information.

When asked about his car or his favourite restaurants, he would reply: "That's personal."

If he thought a question about hockey was dumb, he would say so. He would show signs of a sly sense of humor and poked fun at P.K. Subban, who was his polar opposite in terms of personality.

He would occasionally roll his eyes when Subban got wound up during an interview, but the two developed a bond over the years. Subban was a guest at Markov's 2017 wedding in Moscow.

On one occasion, he talked about a son in Russia who was coming to Canada to play in the famed Quebec peewee tournament.

He expressed his love for Montreal and Canada when he became a Canadian citizen on July 16, 2010.

And we learned about his twin five-year-old sons for the first time when he brought the youngsters to Montreal in 2017 after their mother died of cancer.

Markov played 990 games for the Canadiens and would have topped the 1,000 mark if he hadn't suffered a string of potentially career-ending injuries.

He missed 35 games at the start of the 2009–10 season after a tendon in his leg was cut by Carey Price's skate in the season opener. That season ended with a knee injury in the playoffs against Washington. A series of operations would limit him to 20 games over the next two seasons.

Living the Canadian Dream

One of my favorite Russian players was defenseman Igor Ulanov, a hulking 6-foot-3, 220-pounder whose physical play earned him the nickname the Mangler.

Ulanov felt it was his duty to knock the best opposition player off his game, and his battle with Eric Lindros in the 1996 playoff series between Tampa Bay and Philadelphia is the stuff of legends. Philadelphia won the series in six games, but the punishment

Ulanov inflicted on Lindros was evident in the second round as the Florida Panthers upset the Flyers.

Ulanov played for eight NHL teams and was one of those players who was usually in play at the trading deadline for teams who wanted the missing piece that would push them over the top. Off the ice, Ulanov was a thoughtful, almost gentle character with a sharp sense of humor. While playing for Edmonton, he left a game after being speared in the groin. When a reporter asked him about his condition after the game, he replied: "It's okay, I already have a few kids, I don't need any more."

Ulanov was with the Canadiens for parts of three seasons before being traded to Edmonton at the deadline in 2000. During his stay in Montreal, he became a Canadian citizen.

Ulanov was with the Rangers when the Canadiens visited New York in March 2002, and he talked about how much he enjoyed life in the Big Apple. A week later, the Canadiens were in Florida and were again greeted by Ulanov, who had been traded to the Panthers as part of a blockbuster deal that sent Pavel Bure to the Rangers.

As he discussed the trade with the media, Ulanov said he would miss New York, but, he added: "I'm living the Canadian dream—I get to spend my winters in Florida."

CHAPTER 9
CHARACTER

Le Gros Bill

A light snowfall began in the predawn hours of December 10, 2014, and, by midday, Montreal was in the grips of a fierce winter storm. High winds propelled snow and ice pellets into the faces of pedestrians, but thousands of people lined the streets to watch Jean Béliveau's funeral cortege wind its way from the Bell Centre to Mary Queen of the World Cathedral on Boulevard René Lévesque.

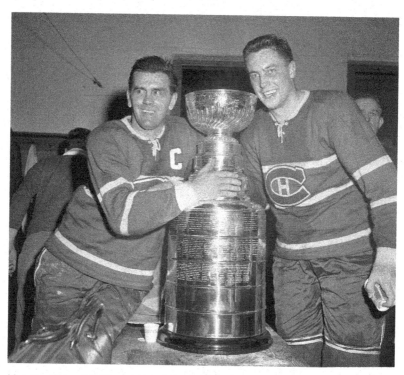

Maurice Richard (left) and Jean Béliveau smile happily in the dressing room with the Stanley Cup after defeating the Boston Bruins 5–3 at the Boston Garden on April 21, 1958. *(AP Photo)*

A steady parade of Montrealers had filed past his body as it lay in state at the Bell Centre for two days, and now it was time to say goodbye. The massive church was filled with his teammates, current players who had been touched by his quiet dignity, politicians, and simple fans who were fortunate to find a place in the crowd.

"You couldn't ask for better weather for hockey or a funeral," a TV reporter said as the wind whipped the hood of his parka.

There might have been better players in the NHL, but nobody matched the respect accorded to Béliveau. The son of a farmer, Béliveau honed his skills playing against factory workers on an outdoor rink in Victoriaville, Quebec.

He moved to Quebec City in 1949 to play junior hockey for the Quebec Citadelles and stayed on to play for the Quebec Aces in the Quebec Senior Hockey League. The Aces filled Le Colisée, and the arena, which was built in 1949, became known as the House that Jean Built.

The Canadiens hoped to bring Béliveau to Montreal, but he was happy in Quebec. When he was a teenager, the Canadiens signed Béliveau to a B form, which required him to play pro hockey for Montreal. Since the Aces were technically an amateur team, the Canadiens couldn't force him to move.

But General Manager Frank Selke was determined to secure Béliveau's services after he joined the Canadiens for a brief trial at the end of the 1952–53 season and scored five goals in three games.

Selke solved the dilemma by buying the entire Quebec Senior Hockey League and changing its designation from amateur to professional.

Béliveau played through the 1970–71 season when he won his 10th Stanley Cup. He became the fourth player to score 500 goals and the second to amass 1,000 points. He won the Hart Trophy as the NHL's most valuable player on two occasions and won the Conn Smythe Trophy as the most valuable player in the 1965 playoffs.

At 6 foot 3 and 205 pounds, Béliveau was an imposing figure on the ice, and he earned the respect of friend and foe alike for the way he matched skill with hard work, a fierce competitive edge with sportsmanship.

After his playing career ended, he held executive positions with the Canadiens and Molson Brewery and was heavily involved in philanthropic work, particularly with the Quebec Society for Disabled Children.

When he retired, the Canadiens marked the occasion with a special ceremony before a game. It was customary on such occasions to shower the player with gifts, but Béliveau received $155,585 to jump-start the Jean Béliveau Foundation. He was also presented with a car equipped to transport children with disabilities.

On his 75th birthday, he was the guest of honor at a $1,000-a-plate dinner at the Bell Centre. That event raised $1 million for the two children's hospitals in Montreal.

On two occasions, Canadian Prime Minister Brian Mulroney offered Béliveau a seat in the Canadian Senate, a position which would have guaranteed him a lifetime of financial security.

Another Canadian prime minister, Jean Chrétien, offered Béliveau the job of governor general, a position as Queen Elizabeth's representative in Canada.

The offer was made in 1994 when Béliveau dined with Chrétien at his official residence in Ottawa. Chrétien told Christopher Curtis of the *Montreal Gazette* that he reached out to Béliveau through a mutual friend, Chrétien's chief of staff and former Quebec City mayor Jean Pelletier. Along with their wives, the three dined together at 24 Sussex Drive on a Tuesday evening in September.

While the group retired to the living room after their meal, Chrétien pulled Béliveau into his study. The former Canadiens captain knew the question was coming before Chrétien asked it.

"Mr. Pelletier told him I'd be making that offer, and unfortunately, for personal reasons, he refused," Chrétien said. "It saddened me, but I understood that he wanted to take care of his family. He was a family man. That was the most important thing to him. He didn't want to become a public figure. I accepted his decision with regret."

Under different circumstances, Béliveau later said, he might have accepted the offer. But after a career that saw him divide much of his time between the Canadiens and his family, Béliveau wanted to be there to help raise his grandchildren, Mylène and Magalie.

Béliveau felt the pull of a family in a tragic crisis: His son-in-law, Serge Roy, a Montreal police officer, had committed suicide a few years before, leaving Béliveau's daughter Hélène as the single mother of two young daughters. Béliveau and his wife, Elise, lived nearby and spent as much time as possible with Hélène and her children. "It was the main reason [I declined]," he said.

"By the time the [governor general]-term was over, our grandchildren would be pretty much grown and independent, another opportunity missed—or so it seemed when I reflected on how quickly my daughter had gone from childhood to young womanhood," Béliveau later wrote of his decision. "Neither Canadian nor Quebec politics, nor partisan sentiment of any kind, had any bearing on my decision."

Béliveau held two auctions of his memorabilia. The first raised nearly $1 million for the Quebec Society for Crippled Children, and a later auction provided funds for his granddaughters' education.

For the most part, Béliveau was relatively apolitical, appealing for calm in Canada's often contentious identity politics. He did hint at his political views in his autobiography, when he said that the Canadiens—a team on which different ethnicities worked toward one goal—were a great metaphor for Canada.

The Canadiens turned to Béliveau to defuse a controversy over the singing of the US national anthem in 2003. Some Canadians were unhappy with the US invasion of Iraq and a friendly fire incident in Afghanistan that killed four Canadian soldiers and wounded eight others.

When the Canadiens played the New York Islanders on March 20, the US anthem was greeted with loud boos. The jeering was featured on network news in the United States, and the Canadiens management felt embarrassed. The Canadiens were home to Carolina two nights later, and team president Pierre Boivin asked Béliveau to address the crowd before the anthem.

"During these difficult times, many have an opinion on world affairs," Béliveau said in the taped message that was shown on the scoreboard screen. "Nevertheless, the Montreal Canadiens have been proud to honor both Canada and the United States prior to games for over 50 years, and they hope to maintain this outstanding display of sportsmanship."

The crowd complied with Béliveau's request. There were a few scattered boos, but they were quickly hushed by most of the crowd. "He had an extraordinary personality," Chrétien said. "You felt his presence in a room. When Béliveau was there, he exuded an atmosphere of respect. He inspired people. That's what inspired me to offer him the post of governor general. People still tell me, 'You made an extraordinary choice; it's too bad he couldn't accept.'"

Chrétien told the *Gazette* he was a law student at Université Laval when he first saw Béliveau play for the Quebec Citadelles in the early 1950s. From that moment, he knew there was something special about the young man from Victoriaville.

"When he played [in Quebec], he was incredible, he was two steps ahead of everyone," Chrétien said. "He was elegant on the ice, he was fast, but didn't look like a fast skater because he had such long legs. For dekeing players, in my sense, to take the puck from behind the net to the other end of the ice, there was him and there was Bobby Orr. Those were the two greatest at that."

Béliveau's later years were marked by health problems. While Béliveau was known for his big-hearted gestures, he had a series of heart problems because his actual heart was relatively small. He survived throat cancer in 2000, although the surgery affected his salivary glands, and he carried a bottle of water wherever he went. He also had several strokes.

As he was laid to rest, former teammate Gilles Tremblay offered this comment: "Jean was so respected. When a fan would see Bobby Hull, he might shout, 'Hey Bobby,' but when people saw Jean, they addressed him as Mr. Béliveau."

The Renaissance Man

Ken Dryden played only seven full seasons in the NHL, but he left an indelible mark on the Canadiens.

He won the Calder Trophy as the rookie of the year in 1972 a year after he won the Conn Smythe Trophy as the most valuable player in the playoffs. He was an integral part of six Stanley Cup teams, and he walked away from the game on his own terms.

That's the way he has lived most of his life, making his mark in the classroom, in politics, and in public service.

Dryden's older brother Dave was also a goaltender, and he took the traditional route to the NHL, playing major junior hockey and working his way through the minor leagues.

Ken was more interested in education, and he spurned an offer from the Canadiens to enroll at Cornell University. He played three seasons for the Big Red, earning All-American honors in each season. In 1967, he was the most valuable player in US college hockey as Cornell became the first Ivy League school to win an NCAA hockey championship.

Dryden joined the Canadian national team after graduation and was pondering his future when the Canadiens made another pitch. They knew Dryden was interested in attending law school, and they had a proposition. The Canadiens' AHL farm team, the Voyageurs, was based in Montreal, and the team would work to accommodate his schedule while he attended law school at McGill University.

The plan was for Dryden to spend the entire season in the AHL, but he was called up to the Canadiens late in the season and posted a 6–0 record with a 1.65 goals against average. Coach Al

Ken Dryden in the net against the Detroit Red Wings at Joe Louis Arena in 1973. *(Malcolm Emmons/USA TODAY Sports)*

MacNeil was so impressed that he decided to start the youngster in the playoffs. Twenty games later, the Canadiens were the Stanley Cup champions. Dryden finished the playoffs with a 3.00 goals against average and was awarded the Conn Smythe Trophy as the playoff MVP. Dryden won his second Stanley Cup in 1973, but he made it clear that hockey was only one part of his life. His contract was up, and he wasn't happy with the Canadiens' offer. With the negotiations at an impasse, the 26-year-old Dryden announced that he was retiring. He moved to Toronto where he spent the year as an articling student, the final step in earning his law degree.

The Canadiens used three different goaltenders in the 1973–74 season, and they all struggled. Montreal finished second in the East Division but was bounced by the Rangers in the first round of the playoffs.

General Manager Sam Pollock went back to Dryden with a revised offer, and the goaltender returned to the fold.

The Canadiens won four consecutive Stanley Cups from 1976 until 1979. Dryden became an iconic figure as he stood in his net and leaned on his stick during breaks in the action.

But 1979 marked the end of an era for the Canadiens with the departures of Dryden, head coach Scotty Bowman, and General Manager Pollock.

Bowman was upset because he wasn't offered the opportunity to replace Pollock, who left to pursue other business opportunities with the Bronfman family, which sold the team to Molson Breweries.

Dryden decided it was time to get on with his life. As he chronicled in his best-selling book, *The Game*, he was losing his enthusiasm for hockey. At the height of his career, he announced his retirement for a second time and made it clear that he wasn't coming back.

Dryden was heavily influenced by his father, Murray. A businessman and philanthropist, Murray Dryden taught his children the value of helping others. Murray was the driving force behind a charity that provided clean bedding for youngsters in underdeveloped countries.

Ken Dryden could have stepped into a lucrative career at any of Canada's leading law firms, but he chose to embark on a series of challenges based on public service.

He was employed as Ontario's youth commissioner, charged with addressing the unemployment problem among young people. He expanded his mandate to look at the high dropout rate among high school students. He quietly left the job after two years. He left behind an 85-page report containing recommendations that were largely ignored by the provincial government.

In an effort to understand the challenges facing youth, he returned to high school as a student and wrote a book about his experiences.

In 2004, he entered politics after resigning as vice-chairman of Maple Leaf Sports and Entertainment, the parent company of the Maple Leafs and Toronto Raptors. He was elected to the Canadian Parliament and served in the House of Commons for seven years. He was a member of Prime Minister Paul Martin's cabinet, serving as minister of social development, and he was among the candidates for the Liberal Party leadership in 2006.

Dryden has written seven books with topics ranging from hockey to Canadian identity. *The Game*, which was a critical and commercial success, is an introspective look at his final season with the Canadiens and stands as the best book written about hockey.

Dryden's latest book, *Game Change*, which was released in 2017, addresses the growing problem of concussions in the NHL. Dryden was inspired by the 2015 death of Steve Montador at the age of 35. Montador suffered a serious concussion while playing for the Chicago Blackhawks, and an examination of his brain showed he was suffering from chronic traumatic encephalopathy (CTE), a degenerative brain disease resulting from concussions.

Dryden proposes a number of radical changes, including a zero-tolerance policy on hits to the head whether intentional or unintentional. He also calls for an end to the practice of players "finishing their checks" and hitting opponents when they are vulnerable after giving up the puck.

Beating the Odds

It was shortly after noon on February 27, 2009, when Glen Metropolit stepped out of the shower in the visitors' dressing room at the Bell Centre and one of the team's equipment managers told him that coach John Stevens wanted to see him.

"I just wanted to let you know that you'll be dressing tonight," said Stevens. "But you'll be dressing for the Canadiens. They just picked you up on waivers."

"Some guys get traded, and they have to rush to the airport to catch a plane, and all I had to do was walk down the hall," said Metropolit.

Metropolit played 407 regular-season games in the NHL, and his last 90 NHL games were played with the Canadiens. He was

34 years old, and his work ethic made him popular with fans and teammates. He played with seven different NHL teams as well as teams in Sweden, Finland, Switzerland, Germany, and Austria. He earned his living as a hockey player into his 40s.

He beat the odds because he was never drafted by the junior Ontario Hockey League or by the NHL. Most of his youth hockey in the Greater Toronto Hockey League was played at the second-tier AA level.

He beat the odds because hockey is expensive, and there was little money—and even less stability—in the Metropolit household growing up.

He never met his biological father, who was a Hells Angels biker when he met Metropolit's mother, Linda. When Glen was growing up, the only time he saw his stepfather, Bruce Metropolit, was when he visited him in jail.

The closest thing to home for Metropolit was Regent Park, a public housing project on the edge of downtown Toronto. But Metropolit said he moved about 50 times before he was 18. He was shuffled between relatives and foster care and was surrounded by drugs and alcohol. As a teenager, he recalled watching hockey games with his uncles while they drank beer and smoked marijuana. He would then join them for adult hockey games at the Moss Park Arena across the street from the housing project.

Hockey was the one stabilizing factor in Metropolit's life. While many of his peers, including his younger stepbrother Troy, found themselves on the wrong side of the law, Glen spent his spare time on one of the two outdoor rinks in the area. When the rinks were closed, he could be seen stickhandling a rubber ball as he walked the streets. He went to church and prayed that he would make it to the NHL, but it seemed a distant dream.

He relied on hand-me-down equipment from friends and played high school hockey and for local AA teams because he lacked the resources to travel and attend summer hockey camps.

When the OHL ignored him, he went to play for the Junior B Richmond Hill Riot. The team, which was located north of the city, might have taken a pass on Metropolit, but a friend on the team vouched for him.

The Junior B exposure led to some interest from US college teams. Bowling Green and UMass Lowell both offered him scholarships, but he ran into problems with the NCAA clearinghouse, which is responsible for certifying athletes before they are eligible to play. There was a core subject missing from his high school record, and his standardized test scores were below the required minimum. The schools were willing to take a chance on him, but the NCAA rules meant that he wouldn't be eligible to play in his freshman year. More significantly, there was no scholarship money for that year.

The college dream ended when Metropolit signed to play roller hockey for the Long Island Jawz, receiving $400 a game. From there, it was on to the life of a hockey nomad, starting in the ECHL and progressing up the ladder to the IHL, the AHL, and, finally in the 1999–2000 season, to his first NHL gig with the Washington Capitals.

While Metropolit was making something of his life, his stepbrother Troy was heading in the opposite direction. Glen and Troy's mother, Linda Hachey, tried to steer Troy into hockey, but coaches found him difficult to handle, and Troy drifted into a childhood marked by truancy and petty crime.

By the time Glen was putting together an 80-point season with the Grand Rapids Griffins, which would open the door to the NHL, Troy had already been sentenced to two 18-month prison terms, the first for robbing a jewelry store and the second for assaulting a police officer and resisting arrest.

On January 6, 1999, Troy joined some friends in what started out as a bump and rob. The idea was to bump into the back of a luxury vehicle and then rob the driver of the car when he got out to survey the damage. This particular caper went wrong when Troy and his friends decided to kidnap the victims, a prominent Toronto lawyer and his wife.

They took the victim back to Regent Park and went from trying to obtain the PIN numbers for their credit cards to demanding a ransom. The couple escaped when Troy and one of the accomplices went to get something to eat and the other member of the gang fell asleep.

Troy was sentenced to 16 years in prison for kidnapping, assault, and forcible confinement.

Glen Metropolit moved to Europe in 2003, and he was playing for Jokerit in Finland when Troy found himself in more trouble. He got into an altercation at the Millhaven penitentiary near Kingston, Ontario, and he stabbed a fellow inmate to death. He was originally charged with first-degree murder, but he pleaded guilty to manslaughter and had eight years added to his sentence.

When he moved to Jokerit, Metropolit figured that he would spend the remainder of his career in Europe, where his speed was an asset on the larger ice surface and he was a fan favorite with his skills and determination. But after leading the Swiss League in scoring with Lugano in 2006, the Atlanta Thrashers offered him another crack at the NHL. He had further stops in St. Louis, Boston, and Philadelphia before landing in Montreal.

Metropolit had his most productive NHL season with the Canadiens in 2009–10. He scored 16 goals and 29 points in 69 games and helped Montreal reach the Eastern Conference Final, where they lost to Philadelphia. He had made a positive contribution to the team, but he was 36 years old, and General Manager Pierre Gauthier wanted to make room for younger players like David Desharnais and Lars Eller. When no other NHL team offered him a job, Metropolit headed back to Switzerland, where he would win two more scoring titles.

Ken Campbell of the *Hockey News* put Metropolit's NHL career in perspective when he noted that 264 players were drafted in 1992, the year Metropolit went unnoticed, and only 40 of them played more NHL games. Only 29 of those players surpassed Metropolit's 89 goals and 34 managed to top his 159 points.

He had a chance for the biggest payday of his career in 2011 when Yaroslavl offered him $1.2 million to play in the KHL. His family was reluctant to make the move, and Metropolit re-signed with Zug in the Swiss League for $400,000. Two months later, an aging aircraft carrying the Yaroslavl team crashed, killing all 44 people on board.

Metropolit spent the 2016–17 season with Bolzano, an Italian team in the Austrian League. He retired in February 2017 at the age of 43.

In 2016, he was reunited with his brother Troy, who was released on parole, and he is helping to support his 83-year-old grandmother and his mother, who is now employed as a bus driver.

The kid who dreamed of life as a pro hockey player left the game with a résumé that included 24 teams spread over 11 leagues in six countries.

CHAPTER 10
CHARACTERS

Author, Author

Terry Ryan found it difficult to step away from the game of hockey.

In the spring of 2014, Ryan was in Dundas, Ontario, for what was supposed to be his swan song. Nineteen years after the Canadiens selected him in the first round (eighth overall) of the 1995 NHL entry draft, Ryan was playing for the Clarenville Caribous, a senior team in his native Newfoundland.

The Caribous were playing the Dundas Real McCoys in the final of the Allan Cup, Canada's national senior championship, but the 37-year-old watched from the stands as his team lost 3–2 in overtime.

Ryan was a few weeks away from being the published author of a memoir—*Tales of a First-Round Nothing*—and he said he took a page out of the book when he decided to bench himself.

"I was suspended for the first game for something that happened back in Newfoundland, but I've had a problem with my ribs for the past two years and I thought it was the best thing for the team if I sat out," Ryan said.

Caribous coach Ivan Hapgood was surprised by Ryan's decision.

"Everybody wants to play," Ryan said. "I've enjoyed playing, but my book is all about sacrifice—well, maybe not all about sacrifice—and I thought it would be best if the other guys played. We won that first game 6–2, and we had five lines worth of forwards. It's not like a few years ago when I was winning scoring titles in our league."

"It's good hockey," the 37-year-old added. "We have some former pros, and each team is allowed four imports."

In this case, imports are players who are not from Newfoundland and Labrador.

The Dundas team that won the title had a few former NHLers of its own. Player-coach Jay McKee had a long career in the bigs, and one of the team's top forwards was Jason Ward, who was the Canadiens' first-round draft pick in 1997 (11th overall).

"It was tough not playing, but it makes a nice bookend to my career," said Ryan.

Ken Dryden's *The Game*, a cerebral journey through his final season in the NHL, is the best book about hockey written by a former Canadien. Ryan's book, an irreverent look at a career that fell far short of Dryden's Hall of Fame credentials, is the funniest book about hockey written by a former Canadien.

Jim Bouton's *Ball Four* was a best seller that chronicled the foibles and misdeeds of his New York Yankees teammates. But Ryan himself is the only player who gets thrown under the bus in his book, which is subtitled: *My Life as an NHL Footnote*.

The ability to laugh at himself is reflected in his answer to the question why he wrote the book.

"I guess I was sick of answering the question 'What happened to your hockey career?'" Ryan said.

He talks candidly about binge drinking, chasing and being chased by women, and a career that went off the rails before it ever got started.

He admits that part of his misfortune was self-inflicted. He rode the thin line between confidence and cockiness, and he alienated the Canadiens' brass.

Part of it was bad luck. A concussion cut short his first stint in the NHL. A high-ankle sprain torpedoed his chances when Dallas was about to give him one last shot.

Ryan's injury woes began before he played his first NHL game. He suffered two serious concussions in the 1995–96 season with the junior Tri-City Americans. He made the Canadiens roster as a 19-year-old in 1996, but his NHL debut was delayed when he discovered that Tie Domi has a hard head. Ryan suffered a hairline fracture in his left hand when he accepted an invitation to fight Domi in a preseason game.

Coach Mario Tremblay, who made his NHL debut as an 18-year-old, said there was no reason to send Ryan back to junior hockey. He said his plan was to use the rookie in 35–40 games. But a bout of tonsillitis followed the hand injury, and Ryan didn't make his NHL debut until October 26, when he played one shift in a 6–5 win over Philadelphia.

He played two more games, but he began to complain of headaches. The original diagnosis was severe migraines, but, after a battery of tests including an MRI, the Canadiens determined that he was suffering from post-concussion syndrome. When he was cleared to resume practicing in late January, he was returned to Tri-City.

The following season, Ryan was the American Hockey League rookie of the year with the Fredericton Canadiens. He had 18 goals and 21 assists while racking up 256 penalty minutes. He led the AHL with 34 fights.

He was recalled to Montreal on three occasions and played four games. He failed to register a point, but he did show off his fighting skills and did his first—and only—interview as a player on *Hockey Night in Canada*.

His first game that season was on January 27. He started on a line with Mark Recchi and Jonas Hoglund but didn't get an opportunity to show off his offensive skill because he collected two minor penalties and a fighting major. His time on the ice—3:32.

In his final appearance of the season in an April 18 home game against Buffalo, he fought Bob Boughner in the first period and Matthew Barnaby in the second. Both fights were free-swinging slugfests with Ryan holding the edge in both scraps. Those fights earned him an interview on *HNIC* where he described the bout against tough guy Barnaby as "the longest of my career or maybe it just seemed that way because it was on TV."

The following season, Ryan played only one game with Montreal, and his frustration was evident at midseason when the Canadiens ran into a series of injuries and looked to the farm for help.

Andrei Bashkirov was called up. So were Matt Higgins and Eric Houde as well as Sylvain Blouin and Dave Morisette, a couple of tough guys in the Ryan mold.

"I truly don't know where I fit in," Ryan said in an interview. "I know anything can happen, and I'm still gunning for Montreal, but I don't know what to expect. I personally don't think I'm [Montreal head coach] Alain Vigneault's type of player."

At one point, Ryan lashed out at Fredericton coach Michel Therrien, resulting in a $250 fine and a seat in the press box for a game. Ryan blamed the incident on stress and depression while Therrien, a noted disciplinarian, said he would continue to push Ryan.

"Sometimes when your kid does something wrong, you talk nice," said Therrien. "If he doesn't change, you become tougher.

But that doesn't mean you don't love the kid. You do it for his own good."

Over the years, Ryan has reflected on a number of what-if scenarios.

"When you join the real world, like I did in 2004 when I became a Red Bull sales rep, which is a pretty good job around here, it was pretty depressing to me at the time because I found that it was not something you love to do," said Ryan.

He said he wrote the book to put his career in perspective.

"Taking away the NHL being the be-all and end-all—now I'm not saying I didn't want to play in the NHL—what I hope people get out of the book is that there's a lot more options to being a successful hockey player than playing in the NHL," Ryan explained.

"People can get their schooling paid for. They can get free travel all over the world, the experience of having the team experience and learning from that."

"I do a lot of hockey schools, and I always get the question, 'What does my boy have to do to make it?'" Ryan said. "No one—zero—ever asks me about the other options.

"Let's say a kid grows up in Windsor watching the Spitfires, and eventually he gets drafted by them," Ryan explained. "That's an accomplishment in itself. He plays on the Windsor Spitfires—as one of my good friends, D.J. Smith, did. If D.J. hadn't gone on to get drafted and if he hadn't gone on to play some NHL games, or be a coach, or even play in the AHL, he could have gotten four years of free schooling. And that's what a lot of people do, and no one talks about it. They act as if it's some sort of failure. And I think it's a great thing."

Ryan went back to school and earned an English degree from Memorial University, and he got to play in the NHL.

"I look at the NHL and the Montreal Canadiens and I laugh and I smile," Ryan said. "I can't believe I was part of that. It's a very positive feeling for me. I'm not ashamed of who I am today. Hockey was a major part of it, and I'm very proud of that. I've got a good life."

In an interview with the *Toronto Star* following the publication of his book, Ryan offered five guidelines for young players:

1. Patience

"If I can say anything to kids coming up it is to be patient. If there was anything I did wrong—and there was a lot of other stuff that was debatable—it was being impatient.

"Time in the minors is good. It can be a good thing. For every Sidney Crosby that does not play in the minors, there is a Jason Spezza that does and learns a lot. Or Corey Perry and Ryan Getzlaf. These guys could have made the same argument I did that they should have played right away. But they played in the minors."

2. Listen to Advice

"It sounds cliché but I would listen to the advice you're being given. The coaches, the trainers, they are all there for a reason."

3. Commit Yourself to Fitness and the Game

"Eat healthy, and work out. You should know that.... The physical demands of hockey, the discipline it takes to stay in and not go to the bar on nights that you shouldn't, it seems like a sacrifice when you're young. But when you're older and you have to work in the real world, it's impossible not to look at your past life as a hockey player with a different set of eyes."

4. Get as Much Money as Quickly as Possible

"My signing bonus was $1.25 million. There is a reason for that. I remember my agent telling me, 'You are one coaching change or GM change away from being buried in Montreal.' And that ended up being true."

5. Enjoy Yourself

"There's a lot more to being a team player than just acting like a soldier. You've got to find the balance, whether you drink or you don't drink. If it was time to go out, whether it's playing cards, or usually it involved going to the bar to pick up women when you're 22 years old, there is a place for that if you do it the right way. There's a place to be social."

At various times, Ryan ignored all those rules, but his biggest mistake was refusing to report to the Canadiens AHL farm club in Quebec City for the 1999–2000 season. Ryan didn't want to play for Therrien, and he signed a minor-league deal with the St. John's Maple Leafs.

He found comfort in going home, but while he was popular in Newfoundland, his ice time was limited. That's because Montreal held his NHL rights and wouldn't trade him. As a result, he wasn't going to get prime playing time ahead of the Leafs' prospects.

While Ryan was off the radar in Newfoundland, the Canadiens went through an incredible string of injuries. Thirty-eight players, including 23 forwards, dressed for the Canadiens that season.

"If I just shut my mouth and had gone back [to Quebec], I know I'd have played in the NHL," said Ryan. "They had a record number of injuries that year, and everybody got called up. All the boys got up. Some guys were getting their first games at 26, 27, 30.

"Knowing what I now know...just be patient."

The Real Estate Magnate

On the ice, Dave Manson was a bruising defenseman with one thing in mind—clear the space in front of the crease. Off the ice, Manson had an engaging personality and a subtle sense of humor.

He spoke in a low, raspy voice, the result of a fight with Sergio Momesso that left him with a damaged larynx, and he was nicknamed Charlie, a reference to cult leader Charles Manson.

He was traded to the Canadiens at the deadline in 1997 and became a popular figure with his teammates. In a series of profiles in the *Montreal Gazette* prior to the 1997–98 season, the players were asked a number of questions including a couple about their vehicles.

"A truck," Manson replied to a query about what he drove.

To a follow-up question about his dream vehicle, Manson replied: "A really big truck."

Manson bought a home in Westmount, an area populated by Montreal's social and financial elite. When asked why he would buy a house in the final year of his contract, Manson replied: "It gives my wife something to do."

At the end of the season, Manson sold the house, and his timing was perfect because there had been a turnaround in the market and he made a tidy profit.

When the Canadiens signed him for the 1998–99 season, he bought another home, but his wife, Lana, didn't get a chance to do much redecorating. Manson was traded to Chicago in mid-November. But again, at least Manson was able to sell the house for a profit.

CHAPTER 11
THE TOUGH GUYS

Hockey's approach to fighting has always been ambivalent. When I worked at the CBC in the early 1970s, the powers that be looked on fighting as an embarrassment. McLaren Advertising owned the rights to televised games in Canada and refused to allow replay of fights. If a news channel wanted to show a fight in its highlights, it had to get permission from McLaren and had to prove there was a legitimate news angle—an injury or a suspension—to justify the replay.

Beginning in 1989, *Hockey Night in Canada* TV commentator Don Cherry made fights a key ingredient in his annual Rock 'Em, Sock 'Em video compilations. More recently, teams have discovered that using a roster spot on a one-dimensional brawler is something they can't afford.

Hockey is still the only team sport that tolerates fighting—the NHL could eliminate fisticuffs if it imposed tougher penalties—and a good fight can still bring fans out of their seats. Fighting is on the decline, but there are some former Canadiens who could have brought that something special to the table, whether they dropped the gloves or not.

The Perfect Fit

Canadiens general manager Frank Selke could see the game of hockey beginning to change in the 1960s. The teams in Montreal were known as the Flying Frenchmen and were built on speed and skill. Their rivals attempted to slow them down with brute force, and Selke feared for the safety of stars like Jean Béliveau. He began to look for someone who could keep the peace, an enforcer.

John Ferguson fights with New York Rangers' Bob Nevin in a 1964 game.
(AP Photo/CP Picture Archive)

He found his man in John Ferguson, a journeyman left winger who was playing for the Cleveland Barons in the American Hockey League. Veteran hockey writer Red Fisher rated the acquisition as one of the top 10 trades in Canadiens' history although the only thing going the other way was a wad of cash. Here's how Fisher described the deal and Ferguson's impact on the team:

"When GM Frank Selke sent scout Floyd Curry to Cleveland, he saw John Bowie Ferguson, with menace implicit in his eyes. What he saw was Ferguson, who had scored 38 goals and 40 assists with the American Hockey League's Barons the preceding season, fire a puck at a teammate's head when he saw him exchanging pleasantries with an opponent during a pregame warmup. He was everything the Canadiens needed. Mean. Intimidating. Unforgiving. He hit people to hurt them. He also played hurt.

"Everyone knew what he stood for during his eight seasons with the team...how he felt, what he thought, liked, loved, and hated. What he loved was to win. Losing was what he hated. There was nothing complicated about his game. It was hit first, ask no questions later. He played to inflict pain...to intimidate. No exceptions. Opposing players were fair game. If he happened to be a goaltender, tough!"

Ferguson is remembered as one of the most feared fighters in NHL history, but, in fact, he was a very good hockey player whose skills as a pugilist were the hockey equivalent of a nuclear deterrent.

He began his NHL career at the relatively late age of 25 as the left winger on a line with Hall of Famers Jean Béliveau and Bernie (Boom Boom) Geoffrion. His main task was to keep opponents from roughing up Béliveau, but he pulled his weight offensively. He played 500 games over eight seasons, and he contributed 145 goals and 158 assists. His best season was 1968–69 when he scored 29 goals and added 23 assists. It was also the season when he spent the most time in the penalty box—185 minutes.

On a team loaded with skilled players—12 of his teammates were elected to the Hall of Fame—Ferguson created his offense with hard work. He was a left-handed shot, but he played most of his career on the right wing.

The Canadiens won the Stanley Cup fives times during Ferguson's tenure, and Béliveau believed Ferguson was a major contributor to that success. In his autobiography, Béliveau wrote that Ferguson was "the most formidable player of the decade and possibly in the Canadiens' history. His greatest contribution was his spirit...his intensity consumed him, his blood boiling when that of others simply simmered."

For all of his reputation as a brawler, it's sometimes difficult to separate fact from the legend. Ferguson once said he aimed to be "the meanest, rottenest, most miserable cuss ever to play in the NHL," but late in life he said he stepped away from the game at age 32 because he feared that he would seriously hurt an opponent.

While Ferguson is remembered as a fighter, he was a fierce checker even though he seldom carried more than 185 pounds on his 6-foot frame. When he fought, he fought with a purpose, to defend a teammate, to right a wrong. He had epic battles with Bobby Hull and Eddie Shack in an era when players didn't wear helmets.

His fight card is remarkably thin. Counting playoffs, he dropped the gloves only 51 times, and he never had more than seven fights in a season.

One of the enduring myths regarding Ferguson is that he made his presence felt immediately upon entering the NHL by fighting Boston Bruins tough guy Ted Green 12 seconds into his very first NHL game. It makes for a great story, but, like many great stories, it doesn't stand up to the facts.

Ferguson did fight Green in his rookie season, but, by the time they fought on January 1, 1964, Ferguson had about a dozen games and an NHL fight under his belt. And the fight broke out at 7:29 of the third period. Ferguson's first NHL fight had been on December 1, 1963, when he took on Boston's Eddie Westfall.

Ferguson had five fights that season, and four of those fights were against Bruins. Boston wasn't very good in those days, finishing last in the six-team league, and the Bruins often figured that their best chance to win was to create mayhem. Ferguson finished his first season with 18 goals and 27 assists in 59 games and was the runner-up to teammate Jacques Laperriere in the Calder Trophy voting for rookie of the year.

Ferguson's work ethic and toughness were forged in his youth. He grew up in the east end of Vancouver near the Pacific National Exhibition grounds, which housed an arena and the Hastings Park racetrack. Ferguson's father died when he was in elementary school, and he worked before and after school to supplement his mother's earnings as a seamstress. He was a stick boy for the junior and minor pro teams that played at the arena, and he mucked the stalls at the track.

There was little time in the young Ferguson's life for play, and he was 11 before he learned to skate. As a teenager, he was better known as a lacrosse player, but the University of Denver thought enough of his hockey ability to offer him a scholarship. Ferguson dreamed of becoming an engineer, but the New York Rangers had different ideas.

In those days, NHL teams routinely signed players to C cards, which bound a player to that team for the rest of their lives or until the team had no further use for him. The Rangers noted that Ferguson's mother had signed such a form for him and that he was ineligible to play college hockey. The NHL team arranged for him to play junior hockey for the Melville Millionaires in the Saskatchewan Junior Hockey League. From there, it was on to the Fort Wayne Komets and the Cleveland Barons. The term journeyman became attached to his name until the Canadiens rescued him.

Ferguson was revered by his teammates, who once voted him as the team's most valuable player. Béliveau offered the following appraisal to authors Chrys Goyens and Allan Turowetz in their book *Lions in Winter*:

"Fergy disrupted the other teams, all over the ice. When he was in the other team's zone, the goalie had to keep an eye on him at all times and that helped the rest of us who were making plays and taking shots. But he was just as valuable off the ice. John hated to lose and the players on his team were afraid of him a bit. With a guy like him on your team, you don't want to fool around. He doesn't have to say anything. All he has to do is look at you, like the Rocket [Maurice Richard] used to do."

Philadelphia's Bobby Clarke broke into the NHL in 1969 and has this recollection of Ferguson's effect: "I was scared to death to be on the ice against him, and he probably even scared his teammates. He was on a line with Pete Mahovlich, who was an easygoin' guy, and John's job was to light a fire under him. The way John yelled at Pete on the ice it must have scared him because it scared all of us on the Flyers. With that beak of his, John looked like a hawk, and he'd burn a hole in you when he looked at you. Everything he did was calculated to unnerve you and give his team the best chance to win the game."

Ferguson collected his fifth Stanley Cup ring in 1971, defeating the Chicago Blackhawks 3–2 in the seventh game of the final. Béliveau announced his retirement after the game.

As they flew back to Montreal after Game 7, Béliveau was sitting next to Ferguson when the enforcer said: "I can't do it anymore. I think I'm going to retire with you." According to Béliveau, one of the toughest players in NHL history had tears in his eyes. General Manager Sam Pollock tried to dissuade Ferguson by offering him a raise and the captaincy, which had been vacated by Béliveau, but Ferguson remained adamant.

He had been playing in an era before big money became part of the game, but Ferguson was making more money outside hockey.

"He had a good head for business," said Gary Ulrich, whose company made high-end children's clothing. "This was before you saw logos on everything, and he suggested that we put the Canadiens logo on our snowsuits. We made a deal with the team, and the suits became one of our biggest sellers."

Ferguson developed a line of turtleneck sweaters, and, for a while, he was the host of a weekly TV show on the CBC. When producer Dale Barnes asked me if I wanted to work as a writer on the *John Ferguson Show*, I assumed that it would be devoted to hockey. I was surprised to learn it was a weekly look at amateur sport with an emphasis on high schools and teenagers. After his death, the *Montreal Gazette* ran a series of letters from fans, and one recounted the times Ferguson joined local youngsters for touch football games.

But his greatest success was as a horseman. His father and his uncle both worked as trainers, and a racetrack in Maryland was the inspiration for his middle name Bowie.

Ferguson had a keen interest in standardbred racing, and, for a while, he handicapped the races at Montreal's Blue Bonnets track for the *Montreal Gazette*. He owned a number of successful horses, and, heeding the advice of prominent breeder Elgin Armstrong, Ferguson began to purchase fillies with breeding potential. At one point he owned 13 mares and nine foals at Hanover Shoe Farms. He eventually sold most of the mares except Lady Kin Hanover, the dam of Merger, which Ferguson bred. Merger was syndicated at the age of two for over $8 million and, as a 3-year-old, won the Little Brown Jug, one of harness racing's Triple Crown races.

As an owner Ferguson's best horse was Hardie Hanover, a winner of stakes events such as the Fan Hanover and Breeders Crown and over $718,000 in purse money. She was voted Canada's 3-Year-Old Pacing Filly of the Year in 1994. Other horses he owned included Stand And Deliver, Caught My Eye, Armbro Income, and Carlys Table. He later became president of Windsor Raceway and helped revive the harness racing industry in Ontario. He was posthumously inducted into the Canadian Horse Racing Hall of Fame in 2016.

But Ferguson wasn't finished with hockey even though he had played his last game. When the Summit Series between Canada and the Soviet Union was announced, Team Canada coach Harry Sinden offered Ferguson a spot on the team even though he hadn't played in more than a year. Ferguson declined, but Sinden was determined to have him involved. Sinden offered him a job as assistant coach, hoping that his competitiveness would serve as an inspiration for his all-star lineup.

Ferguson's presence may have been the key to Team Canada's come-from-behind victory in the historic series.

In Game 6, the Soviets were on the verge of clinching the series, and, as Ferguson told the story, he asked Bobby Clarke to take out the Soviets' best player, winger Valeri Kharlamov. "I called Clarke over to the bench, looked at Kharlamov and said, 'I think he needs a tap on the ankle,'" he once said. "I didn't think twice about it. It was us versus them, and Kharlamov was killing us. I mean somebody had to do it."

Clarke remembers the story a little differently.

"Fergie just said, 'We gotta take that guy outta the game,'" Clarke said. "He didn't say it to me directly. I was standing by the bench when he said it, but he made sure that the right guys would hear it. He couldn't have known who'd have a chance to do something about it. He never said to break Kharlamov's ankle. He was only asking us to do something that he would have done himself."

A few shifts later, Clarke did break a bone in Kharlamov's ankle with a slash, and the series turned in Canada's favor. Kharlamov returned for the eighth and deciding game of the series, but he was ineffective. While Clarke's teammate Paul Henderson and others have questioned the ethics of the slash, Clarke and Ferguson never voiced any regrets or doubts.

The Summit Series was an eye-opener for North Americans. The skill of the Soviet players showed that Canada wasn't the only place that produced great hockey players. Ferguson recognized this and put that knowledge to good use as an executive with the New York Rangers, the Winnipeg Jets, and the Ottawa Senators.

Dallas Stars general manager Jim Nill played for Ferguson in Winnipeg and later scouted with him in the Senators' organization. He told journalist Gare Joyce there was a case to be made for Ferguson's place in the Hockey Hall of Fame.

"Fergie was the tough guy's tough guy as a player, but he appreciated skill and had a great eye for it," said Nill. "He was the one who found Thomas Steen and Teemu Selanne. It was Fergie who pushed us in Ottawa to draft Daniel Alfredsson and Pavol Demitra in the later rounds. He wasn't just a good hockey man. He was way ahead of the curve. If he didn't go into the Hockey Hall of Fame as a player, you could make a heck of a case for him as a builder."

Ferguson spent parts of two seasons as head coach of the Rangers and then became general manager. The Rangers didn't enjoy much success in those years, but he did pull off a coup when he lured Anders Hedberg and Ulf Nilsson away from the Winnipeg Jets of the World Hockey Association. The Swedes were among the best players in the WHA.

That move had an ironic twist. When he was fired by the Rangers in 1978, he became the general manager of the Jets, who were absorbed into the NHL a year later.

When he worked for the Ottawa Senators in the early 1990s as director of player personnel, he was credited with finding Daniel Alfredsson and Alexei Yashin. Ferguson was diagnosed with prostate cancer in 2005 and died two years later at age 68.

Boston's Gift to Montreal

Chris Nilan had 315 fights in his NHL career, but the player who earned the nickname Knuckles never set out to be a brawler.

"I grew up in Boston and, like every kid my age, I wanted to be Bobby Orr," said Nilan. "I wanted to be the guy flying through the air after scoring that goal. At the same time, I'd go to the

Garden to watch the Bruins play, and they had a reputation for playing tough, physical hockey."

Nilan didn't start playing hockey until he was eight years old.

"The first time I skated was on an outdoor rink that was always melting, but the city started building these indoor rinks as a way to keep the kids off the street. There was one at the end of my street, and I did a lot of public skating before I played hockey," said Nilan.

He played at Catholic Memorial High School and Northwood Prep in Lake Placid before enrolling at Northeastern University. Fighting is discouraged in US college hockey, but Nilan learned to fight on the streets of West Roxbury. "I didn't go looking for fights, but I'd stand up for my friends or if someone was bullying a smaller kid. That was something I learned from my father. He was a Green Beret, and their motto was 'Free the oppressed.'"

Nilan was drafted by the Canadiens in the 19th round in 1978, and, a year later, he was in the Nova Scotia Voyageurs training camp.

"They brought Bert Templeton in to coach the team, and he didn't like college guys," said Nilan. "A guy named Rich Costello messed up a drill, and Bert started yelling: 'Costello, you messed up the drill, and now we have to start all over. I thought college guys were supposed to be smart.'

"I was on a five-day tryout, and I was paid $200 a game. My first game was against Maine, and they had manhandled the Vees in the first round of the playoffs the year before. I went out and gave Glen Cochrane a pretty hard check. He went back at me and the gloves came off. I got a good shot in and cut him, and he got madder when the blood started gushing, but I held my own. The next day, Bert called me in and asked me who my agent was. I told him I didn't have one, and then he told me I should call the Canadiens because they wanted to sign me. One fight, that's all it took."

A year later, he was in Montreal.

"When I first went to camp with the Vees, I still had that Boston mentality," said Nilan. "The Canadiens were the enemy, and I hated the players, I hated the organization, I hated everyone. But when I arrived in Montreal, they made me feel so welcome. I stayed at Serge Savard's home my first season. Guy Lafleur, Bob Gainey—they were so helpful."

Nilan was an enforcer in the John Ferguson tradition. He didn't go looking for fights, but he didn't back down when he was challenged and he was quick to retaliate if he felt someone took liberties with one of his teammates. He was proud of his role on a checking line with Gainey and Guy Carbonneau.

"I remember talking with Ken Linseman, and he said we were the toughest line he ever played against," said Nilan. "He said we were the perfect line because we could defend, we could hit, we could score, and we could fight."

Jean Perron broke up the perfect line in the 1987–88 season, and Nilan's unhappiness with the coach increased when the coach suggested that Nilan wasn't fighting enough. The friction between Nilan and Perron resulted in Nilan being traded to the Rangers in January 1988.

"I never had to be told when to fight," said Nilan. "In fact, Jacques Lemaire once told me that he was concerned that I was fighting too much."

That was the 1984–85 season when Nilan established career highs for goals (21) and assists (16) as well as penalty minutes (358).

Nilan returned to finish his career with the Canadiens at the tail end of the 1991–92 season. His 315 fights rank third in NHL history behind Tie Domi with 328 and Dave (Tiger) Williams with 327. He's ninth on the all-time penalty list with 3,043 minutes.

Hockey took its toll on Nilan's body, but he said little of the damage was the result of fighting.

"I had a broken nose and I took a shot to the jaw, but most of the damage I suffered was structural," said Nilan, who has had surgery to repair his knees and an ankle. "I've had concussions, but if they find out I had CTE after I die, I'd like to think it was because of the car accident I had where I was thrown from the vehicle and they found me lying on the side of the road."

Nilan's attempts to deal with pain after his hockey career ended in substance abuse and a heroin addiction. He has been sober for more than a decade and has been involved in numerous efforts to combat drug abuse. He has shared his story in an autobiography *Fighting Back*, and he was the focal point of *The Last Gladiators*, a documentary about fighting in the NHL.

Nilan is currently the host of *Off the Cuff*, a daily radio show on TSN–690 in Montreal. He provides listeners with insights from the perspective of a former player and doesn't back off from controversy. Considering the way he made his living, it's interesting to hear his perspective on fighting in today's NHL.

"I don't care if I never see another hockey fight," Nilan said. "I say that because I've been a fighter and I've seen what it can do. And in today's game, everybody's got a visor and you can mess up your hands. It's stupid. I think most of the concussion problems are the result of things other than fighting, but it just doesn't make sense."

Nilan said his current view of fighting was influenced by a scrap between George Parros of the Canadiens and Toronto's Colton Orr in the season opener on October 1, 2013. Parros, an articulate Princeton graduate who was nearing the end of his career, lost his balance and fell face-first on the ice. He was taken to the Bell Centre clinic on a stretcher and diagnosed with a concussion.

"I was in the press box right above the action, and I felt sick," said Nilan.

Nilan also has some views on the way the game is played today.

"There are too many long passes," he noted. "You don't see players coming back to support the rush as a team. Everybody wants to score because that's how they get paid."

The Quebecois Hoosier

Montreal Gazette colleague Stu Cowan received a huge surprise the first time he met Donald Brashear.

"I was at the Canadiens training camp, and I noticed this big black guy who was hitting everybody," recalled Cowan. "I looked at the lineup and saw that his name was Donald Brashear and he was from Bedford, Indiana. My first thought was that he should be playing basketball, not hockey, and I figured that there had to be a story there.

"When the practice ended, I went to the dressing room and introduced myself, and then I discovered that he didn't speak English very well," said Cowan.

That was because Brashear had lived most of his life in Quebec speaking French. His mother, Nicole Gauthier, is a white French-Canadian and his father, Johnny Brashear, is a black American. Brashear was serving in the United States Air Force at a radar station in St. Albans, Vermont, when he met Nicole on a visit to Montreal.

They moved to his hometown in Indiana and settled into a domestic relationship that was anything but idyllic. Johnny Brashear was an abusive alcoholic, and his wife left him and their three children when Donald, the youngest, was barely a year old. She returned a few months later to collect her two older kids, but Donald remained in Indiana until he was five years old.

Johnny Brashear abused his son, whipping him with a belt or electrical wire, and he was traumatized by the time he was reunited with his mother.

Nicole Gauthier had remarried and said Donald's reunion with his family didn't go well. She told the *Washington Post* that her new husband wasn't enthused over having another mixed-race child in the household. He would berate Donald for not being able to tie his shoes, and the youngster was forced to wear a garbage bag at night because he wet the bed.

Donald's relationship with his mother was also strained. He resented her for having abandoned him, and, after two tumultuous years, Donald was placed into the foster-care system. He got lucky with his second placement.

"I was placed in a family with three boys and a girl, and they all played hockey," said Brashear. "It was a very loving environment."

Brashear thrived as a hockey player. He played midget hockey near his new home in Quebec and then moved to Montreal to play three seasons with Collège Français in the Quebec Major Junior Hockey League. He was overlooked in the NHL entry draft, but the Canadiens signed him as a free agent in 1992.

By this time, Brashear was 6 foot 2 and weighed more than 200 pounds. He had 18 goals and 24 assists in his final season of junior hockey, but the number that caught General Manager Serge Savard's eye was his 288 penalty minutes.

Over 16 NHL seasons, Brashear developed a reputation for being one of the most feared fighters in the league, but he took pride in the fact that he was a hockey player. While playing for the Canadiens' farm club in Fredericton in 1993–94, he established his professional highs with 38 goals and 66 points in 62 games while also racking up 250 penalty minutes.

He played parts of four seasons with the Canadiens, but his stay in Montreal ended on November 9, 1996, when he got into a shouting match with head coach Mario Tremblay who, a year earlier, had been on the receiving end of Patrick Roy's wrath. The argument was caught on tape by RDS cameraman Paul Buisson and General Manager Réjean Houle felt that he couldn't allow players to challenge the coach's authority. Four days later, Brashear was traded to Vancouver.

After leaving Montreal, Brashear was involved in two of the ugliest incidents in NHL history.

It was business as usual for Brashear on February 21, 2000, when he was playing for the Vancouver Canucks. He got into a fight with Boston Bruins enforcer Marty McSorley, who was on the downside of his career after once serving as Wayne Gretzky's protector with the Edmonton Oilers. Brashear handily won the fight and couldn't resist taunting the Bruins' bench as he headed to the penalty box. The Bruins were further incensed later in the game when Brashear collided with Boston goaltender Byron Dafoe. The goaltender suffered a knee injury and was taken off the ice on a stretcher.

McSorley spent the remainder of the game unsuccessfully attempting to goad Brashear into a rematch. With 4.6 seconds remaining in the game, McSorley struck Brashear with a two-handed slash to the head with his stick. Brashear collapsed to the ice, and his helmet fell off upon impact. He suffered a seizure on the ice, and the slash resulted in a grade III concussion.

McSorley was ejected with 2.8 seconds left in the game and later received an indefinite suspension from the NHL. But that was only the start of his troubles. In early March, Vancouver police charged him with assault with a weapon.

The resultant trial in British Columbia was a public relations nightmare for the NHL, which felt that the league was in the best position to deal with disciplinary matters. Bill Daly, who was then in charge of legal affairs for the NHL, felt the league adequately dealt with the issue when it suspended McSorley.

McSorley testified that he tried to hit Brashear in the shoulder to start a fight with him, but missed, resulting in the head shot.

"Don't get me wrong...I feel incredibly bad that Donald Brashear got hurt because of my stick," McSorley said after he was charged. "I wanted him to turn around and have a confrontation with me and fight, like we did earlier in the game, like we've done in games before, and like I've done so many times before."

McSorley was found guilty but avoided a jail sentence. He was required to complete 18 months of probation in which he was not allowed to play in a game against Brashear.

That proved to be a moot point. While Brashear returned to play before the end of the season and finished the season with a career-high 11 goals, McSorley missed the remaining 23 games of the regular season. He had his indefinite suspension officially set at one year following the conviction, but he never played in another NHL game.

Brashear was among the NHL leaders in penalty minutes while playing for the Philadelphia Flyers in the 2003–04 season. He had 212 minutes, including 34 for his role in the most penalized game in NHL history. The Flyers were leading the Ottawa Senators 5–2 on March 5, 2004, when Brashear fought Ottawa enforcer Rob Ray with 1:45 remaining in the game. The fight was believed to be in retaliation to Flyers forward Mark Recchi being slashed in the face by the Senators Martin Havlát. While Brashear and Ray were the main event, five other fights broke out. When the referees restored order, they handed out 419 penalty minutes.

Brashear played 1,025 regular-season NHL games and scored 85 goals and 120 assists. He had 2,634 penalty minutes and would have had more if opponents weren't reluctant to fight him.

Georges Laraque, a career enforcer who retired from the NHL in 2010, described Brashear as "the best. Guys didn't want to fight him because they knew they would be in trouble."

Brashear finished his NHL career with 237 fights, and, in 2000, the *Hockey News* proclaimed him the enforcer of the decade.

Like many enforcers, Brashear is quiet and well-spoken off the ice. The man who was thought to have an intellectual disability as a child has mastered English and can also speak Russian and Spanish. He plays piano and taught himself to play guitar.

He has been a partner in a home construction business and, more recently, began selling hockey sticks under the Brash87 label. He and his partner appeared on *Dragon's Den*, a CBC television show that hooks up budding entrepreneurs with venture capitalists. Three of the panellists were wooed by Brashear's vision of providing high-quality, low-priced sticks and invested $500,000 in the venture.

And here's a note for trivia buffs: Brashear's great-uncle, Carl Brashear, was the first African American to be certified as a master diver in the United States Navy. He was portrayed by Cuba Gooding Jr. in the movie *Men of Honor*.

Life Among the Goons

There was one time in Donald Brashear's career when he was a reluctant fighter.

During the 2004–05 lockout, many NHL players from Quebec returned home to play in Le Ligue Nord-Américaine de Hockey (LNAH), a barely professional league that was referred to as the "goon league."

The LNAH provided some decent hockey sandwiched between two outbreaks of mayhem. Each team carried two or three players whose sole purpose was to fight. Because the league rules called for the ejection of any player who fought twice in a game, there were fisticuffs early in the game and the goons would sit on the bench until the third period when they would again drop the gloves.

The format lent itself to some strange incidents. Link Gaetz, whose brief career as an enforcer with the San Jose Sharks—326 penalty minutes in 48 games in 1991–92—earned him the nickname the Missing Link, played for Thetford Mines Prolab during the lockout.

After fighting in the first period and sitting through the second, he felt the need for some refreshment. He ambled over to the concession stand, grabbed a hamburger, and returned to the bench.

Coach Guy Chouinard, who once had a 50-goal season with the Atlanta Flames, was not amused and tossed Gaetz off the team.

Brashear joined the Radio X team in his hometown of Quebec City, receiving a reported $300,000 for his services. He made it clear that he was there to play hockey and not to fight.

That message was lost on the league's full-time goons. While Brashear was scoring 18 goals and 50 points in 47 games, he was constantly being challenged by fighters hoping to make their reputation and he racked up 260 penalty minutes, a decent total but behind Radio X's fulltime goons, Jacques Dubé and Jason Boily, who topped 300 minutes. Brashear complained that the league wasn't doing enough to protect its better players.

Midway through the season, Radio X came to Montreal to play the Verdun Dragons at the Bell Centre. Brashear was the main draw for the more than 12,000 fans, but he refused to fight.

When the game was over, Dino Marchitello, a local boxing promoter who was also co-owner and assistant coach of the Dragons, stood outside the Radio X dressing room and launched an obscenity-laden and racist tirade at Brashear for not putting on a show for the fans.

When the teams met a week later in Quebec City, the Dragons exacted their revenge by refusing to fight.

The Reluctant Fighter

For the better part of a decade, Georges Laraque was the unofficial heavyweight champion of the NHL, but, by the time he reached the Canadiens in 2008, he wasn't feared as much as he was earlier in his career.

Laraque was excited when he signed a three-year, $4.5-million contract with the Canadiens, and, to this day, he insists that playing in Montreal is one of the highlights of his life even though the Canadiens cut him roughly 18 months after the signing.

General Manager Bob Gainey said he had no regrets about the deal when he cut Laraque loose on January 22, 2010. The Canadiens said they would honor the second year of Laraque's contract but bought out the third year.

Gainey felt the Canadiens needed Laraque because the team had been bullied by the Philadelphia Flyers in the second round of the 2008 playoffs. The Canadiens needed someone to stand up for the team's smaller players.

Unfortunately for the Canadiens, Laraque wasn't the guy. The Canadiens needed someone to react to the playground bully, and Laraque was reluctant to do that unless the bully was a fellow heavyweight.

While he was plagued with injuries during his season and a half with the Canadiens, he had only 13 fights, and they were all against heavyweights. His dance card included fights against Riley Cote, Mitch Fritz, Andrew Peters, Shawn Thornton, and Colton Orr.

Laraque's teammates were reluctant to criticize his approach to picking and choosing his opponents. They talked about the difficulty of being an enforcer. They said the instigator rules make it difficult to seek retribution if you don't have a willing partner.

But defenseman Josh Gorges conceded there were times when a player had to risk taking the extra two minutes that go with being an instigator.

"I know that he didn't want to put the team in jeopardy by taking an extra penalty," Gorges said of Laraque. "His intentions were good in that sense, but there are times when it's okay to take a penalty now and then to send a message, and the rest of us, as a team, have to bail him out and kill that penalty for him."

Gorges noted that players work extra hard to kill those kinds of penalties.

"When you see a teammate go out there and take a penalty for the good of the team, then it's the PK's job to kill that penalty," Gorges said. "That's the whole part of a team, sticking together. If he's sticking up for us, we have to help him."

Laraque said head coach Jacques Martin didn't like him and didn't appreciate toughness. Martin dismissed the allegation, saying he has coached many players and styles during his 25-year NHL coaching career.

Martin didn't give Laraque a lot of ice time. He averaged a shade under six minutes a game, and he sat out 23 games, although it was difficult to know when he was a healthy scratch and when he was suffering from one of his chronic knee or back ailments.

But Larque's ice time reflected his ability—or lack thereof. He was a fourth-liner whose role was defined by his skills. His most obvious skill was his ability to throw punches.

Fourth-liners have to understand and accept their role, and when they don't, they tend to whine and become a distraction in the room. One teammate complained that the media spent a disproportionate amount of time interviewing Laraque. But Laraque was a favorite with reporters because he was well-spoken in both French and English and wasn't afraid to express strong opinions. Laraque was one of the most interesting and most complicated players I've met. The son of Haitian immigrants, he said he had a good childhood despite encountering some racism. He attended Collège Brebeuf, a private Jesuit high school which catered to the children of Montreal's French elite.

He has an engaging sense of humor and a social conscience, which, he admits, was at odds with his chosen profession.

"What I do on the ice is definitely not the type of person I am off the ice," Laraque wrote on his website. "I hate violence. I'm a perfectionist, a bit stubborn and obsessive-compulsive disorder, which is known to drive people crazy, buy hey, we can't all be perfect. I'm a down-to-earth guy.... And also I can pretty much say that my circle of friends is a good reflection of me. They are all positive people that enjoy life. My best friends are just normal, hardworking people who work like the majority of people from 9:00 AM to 5:00 PM."

Laraque is known for his willingness to go into the community and support charitable efforts. After the Canadiens dropped him, he redirected his energy to supporting victims of the 2010 earthquake in Haiti. He partnered with World Vision and the NHL Players Association to support Grace Children's Hospital in Haiti.

Closer to home in Quebec, Laraque is involved with the MIRA Foundation, which provides guide dogs for the visually impaired, and lent his name to groups promoting cancer research, ethical treatment of animals, and anti-bullying efforts. From 2010 to 2013, he was one of the deputy leaders of the Green Party in Canada.

He is probably the city's best-known vegan, although one fund-raising effort backfired on him. He appeared in an online commercial for an "energy" drink that combined the buzz of caffeine and alcohol. Laraque said that when he agreed to do the ad, in return for a contribution to one of his favorite charities, he didn't know it would involve a street hockey game with a cast of scantily clad women. An embarrassed Laraque said he had been brought up to respect women and asked the drink company to pull the ad.

The Fight that Wasn't

Canadiens defenseman Lyle Odelein and Kelly Chase were good friends. Odelein grew up in Quill Lake, Saskatchewan (population 409) while Chase is from Porcupine Plain (population 855). The towns are separated by 120 kilometers of prairie, but in rural Saskatchewan, that qualifies as neighbors.

Odelein and Chase developed a friendly rivalry through minor hockey and later when they graduated to the Western Hockey League. Odelein played for Moose Jaw and Chase was in Saskatoon, and they dropped the gloves on a regular basis.

There was every reason to be believe that the two would renew their physical rivalry on October 27, 1995, when the Canadiens played the Whalers at the Hartford Civic Center.

The prospects of a Chase-Odelein scrap arose after the morning skate when Odelein was talking to Daryl Reaugh, the former goaltender who was the analyst for the Whalers' cable-TV package.

Odelein inquired about Chase's health and, when Reaugh told Odelein that Chase had been in fights in the Whalers' three previous games, Odelein said: "Well, I guess we'll be going tonight."

Odelein then displayed the back of his T-shirt, which pictured a pair of hockey gloves hanging like boxing gloves and the legend "Ya gonna drop 'em or are your gloves glued to your hands?"

Chase also seemed to be looking forward to a scrap. After the morning skate, he talked about his strange friendship with Odelein and about his role as a fighter. He said he was willing to drop gloves with anyone and the player who worried him was Montreal defenseman Vladimir Malakhov.

"He's a beast," Chase said of the 6-foot-3, 227-pound Russian. "He was one of the strongest guys in the league and nobody wants to tangle with him."

That's probably the reason why Malakhov played 14 seasons in the NHL and had only 15 fights.

But referee Andy Van Hellemond eliminated the possibility of a Chase-Odelein matchup after a wild first-period brawl that started with a fight between Chase and Donald Brashear.

Van Hellemond and friends were just getting that one under control when Odelein started fighting with Mark Janssens, and Turner Stevenson took on Glen Featherstone. The latecomers—Odelein, Stevenson, Featherstone, and Janssens—were all asked to take the rest of the night off as they were assessed majors and game misconducts for joining the fray.

CHAPTER 12

THE MEN BEHIND THE BENCH

I had one of those fly-on-the-wall moments in the hours after the 1994 NHL entry draft in Hartford. I was scheduled to fly home at 6:00 PM and Pat Burns, who was coaching the Toronto Maple Leafs at the time, offered to drive me from the Montreal airport to my home in Quebec's Eastern Townships.

We arrived at the airport to discover that our flight was delayed by bad weather. There were torrential rains accompanied by thunder and lightning, and the conditions weren't suitable for the small puddle jumper used on the Hartford-Montreal run. Air Canada was arranging for a larger plane and was rerouting passengers through Boston, but the aircraft wouldn't arrive in Hartford until 9:00 PM.

We decided to wait out the storm in the bar where we met New Jersey Devils coach Jacques Lemaire. Burns and Lemaire had one thing in common—they had both coached the Canadiens— and they spent a couple of hours reflecting on the difficulties associated with the job.

They talked about the pressure, the high expectations that came with guiding a franchise that took winning the Stanley Cups for granted. They talked about dealing on a daily basis with a media horde that was growing exponentially with each season.

Both men would go on to win Stanley Cups with the Devils, but they both walked away from the job in Montreal.

Lemaire, who had a Hall of Fame career as a player with the Canadiens, replaced Bob Berry late in the 1983–84 season. He reached the Eastern Conference Final in 1984 but quit after his first full season behind the bench.

Burns reached the Stanley Cup Final with the Canadiens as a rookie NHL coach in 1989 but quit three years later, citing his frustration over dealing with the media.

If you go back and listen to the coaches when they were first hired, you'll hear a lot of talk about how lucky they are to land the best job in the world. It doesn't always work out that way in the end.

No Experience Required

Finding the right head coach for the Canadiens can be one of the most difficult jobs in professional sport.

When most teams are searching for a coach, they cast a wide net. They can look for a veteran coach with a proven track record. If they have a young team, they can look for a coach with a reputation for developing talent. Or maybe they will take a flyer on the young coach who has been described as the next Scotty Bowman.

In other words, they look for the best available coach.

When the Canadiens have a head coaching vacancy, they look for the best available coach who can speak French.

This requirement hasn't always gone over well with the fan base, particularly those whose first language is English. They point to elite soccer teams in Europe, which regularly hurdle the language barrier when looking for coaches.

But that argument doesn't hold much sway with the Canadiens management. Fifteen different men have been hired to coach the Canadiens since Bowman walked away from the job in 1979, and 13 of them have been fluent in French. A 14th, Bob Berry, could stumble along while Randy Cunneyworth, the interim coach for part of the 2011–12 season, was hopelessly unilingual.

Because the coaching pool is limited, there have been suggestions that the Canadiens do more to develop French-speaking coaches, but, in fact, the team has done that in the past and the Canadiens' coaching job has become an apprenticeship for coaches on their way to bigger and better things.

Nine of those 15 coaches experienced their first NHL head coaching jobs with the Canadiens, and one of them—Mario Tremblay—jumped into the job with no coaching experience at any level.

Two of the coaches who learned on the job—Jacques Lemaire and Pat Burns—went on to win Stanley Cups with the New Jersey Devils, while Alain Vigneault has taken the Vancouver Canucks and the New York Rangers to the Stanley Cup Final.

The Canadiens have won the Cup twice since Bowman's departure, and the man behind the bench for the most recent win in 1993 was Jacques Demers, a career coach who was the head coach of the Quebec Nordiques, St. Louis Blues, and Detroit Red Wings before coming home to Montreal.

The other coach to win a Stanley Cup in the post-Bowman era was Jean Perron, who won in his first year as an NHL head coach. He had been a successful coach in the Canadian university ranks, and Serge Savard recognized his potential. The plan was for Perron to learn how to be an NHL coach as an assistant to Lemaire. Perron's rise to the top was accelerated after Lemaire quit in 1985, and Perron took the top job with one season of pro experience.

Two coaches returned to Montreal for second acts. Michel Therrien was fired by the Canadiens in 2003 but was rehired in 2012 after achieving some success in the Pittsburgh Penguins organization.

Claude Julien was replaced by Bob Gainey in 2006 and went on to win a Stanley Cup in Boston. When the Bruins fired him in 2017, the Canadiens made room for him by dumping Therrien.

The Worst Coach Ever?

That's the way Henri Richard described Al MacNeil during the Canadiens' surprise run to the Stanley Cup in 1971, but there's an argument to be made that MacNeil did a pretty good job in his brief tenure behind the Canadiens' bench.

MacNeil, who logged 11 successful seasons as an NHL player, was coaching the Montreal Voyageurs, the Canadiens' American Hockey League farm club, when he received a surprise phone call from General Manager Sam Pollock.

The Canadiens were off to a lackluster 11–8–4 start and head coach Claude Ruel decided to step down. Ruel had guided the Canadiens to a Stanley Cup in 1969, but he never felt comfortable behind the bench. He was an outstanding judge of talent and took delight running practices, where he exhorted his players to "Skate, skate, skate, shoot, shoot, shoot."

But Ruel had succeeded the legendary Toe Blake, and there was a ton of pressure to win. The Canadiens missed the playoffs in 1970, and the expectations weighed heavily on Ruel. He was happy to return to scouting, although he observed the Canadiens from a distance and occasionally offered advice to his successor.

MacNeil was a novice in the coaching game. He spent one season as a player and head coach with the Houston Apollos of the Central Hockey League and then played a similar role in the 1969–70 season when the Canadiens moved their AHL farm club from Cleveland to Montreal. He hung up his pads after that season to concentrate on coaching. When the Canadiens called, he was 35 years old and many of the Montreal players knew him as a former teammate or rival.

Three players—captain Jean Béliveau, J.C. Tremblay, and Henri Richard—were his teammates when MacNeil played for the Canadiens in the 1961–62 season. And Pierre Bouchard and Guy Lapointe played with, and for, MacNeil in the minors.

Under MacNeil, the Canadiens survived the mediocre start and finished third in the East Division, although they were 24 points behind the powerhouse Boston Bruins. Boston was led by legendary defenseman Bobby Orr, who collected a career-high 139 points. Phil Esposito led the team with 152 points, while linemates Johnny Bucyk and Ken Hodge also topped 100 points.

The Bruins were the defending champions and clear favorites to win the Stanley Cup.

By the time the Canadiens reached the playoffs, they were a different team from the one MacNeil inherited.

Pollock bolstered the offense by acquiring Frank Mahovlich from the Detroit Red Wings midway through the season. Mahovlich was a quiet, brooding player. At 6 foot 1 and 205 pounds, he wouldn't be considered a big player by today's standards, but in the 1960s and 1970s, he was an imposing figure and earned the nickname the Big M. He made the game look easy, and that created a problem because fans looked at his effortless stride and thought he was not working hard. He helped Toronto win four Stanley Cups, but he was overcome by the pressure of trying to please the demanding fan base. On two occasions, he was treated in the hospital for tension and depression.

He welcomed a trade to Detroit in 1968, but the Red Wings were at the bottom of the East Division in the 1970–71 season and the trade to a contender was accompanied by a chance to be reunited with his younger brother Peter. Ironically, Peter Mahovlich was nicknamed the Little M, even though he was taller and heavier than Frank.

Frank Mahovlich had 17 goals and 41 points in 38 games with the Canadiens, but it was his playoff performance that earned him a new battalion of fans. He was the team's offensive leader with 14 goals and 13 assists in 20 games.

Heading into the playoffs as a decided underdog, MacNeil decided he had nothing to lose by starting a rookie goaltender named Ken Dryden. Rogie Vachon had done the heavy lifting during the regular season with Phil Myre as his backup. They did an adequate job, but most observers felt that it wouldn't be good enough in the playoffs where there would be tighter checking and a greater emphasis on defense.

MacNeil had seen Dryden up close earlier in the season when he was coaching the AHL Voyageurs. Dryden, who had been an outstanding goaltender and student at Cornell University, had signed with the Canadiens on the condition that they would allow him to combine hockey with law school at McGill University. Because of his demanding schedule, the plan was to keep him in the AHL for the entire season. But the Canadiens recalled Dryden late in the season, and he posted a 6–0 record with a 1.65 goals against average.

That brief introduction to the NHL convinced MacNeil that it was time to roll the dice and start the 6-foot-4 Dryden in the opening round of the playoffs against the Bruins.

Boston won the opening game 3–1 and was leading 5–1 in Game 2 when the Canadiens came to life. Montreal took advantage of some uncharacteristic mistakes from the overconfident Bruins and rallied for a 7–5 win. The Canadiens would go on to win the series in seven games. It was a stunning upset made more impressive because three of the four Montreal wins, including a 4–2 victory in Game 7, came at the Boston Garden.

The Canadiens defeated the Minnesota North Stars in a six-game series to qualify for the Stanley Cup Final against the Chicago Blackhawks.

The Canadiens lost the first two games of the final in Chicago. When things started getting away from the Canadiens in Game 2, MacNeil started shuffling his lines and, at one point, he benched veteran Henri Richard.

The younger brother of Maurice (Rocket) Richard was upset to find himself glued to the bench for an extended period. He and MacNeil had their differences during the season, but, on this occasion, Richard went public with his unhappiness. After the game, he told reporters that MacNeil was the worst coach that he ever played for.

By the time the team arrived in Montreal for Game 3, MacNeil has been anointed as public enemy No. 1 by thousands of French-Canadian fans. MacNeil was already persona non grata among many fans because he didn't speak French, although he was planning to take French classes in preparation for the 1972–73 season.

The anti-MacNeil backlash was so strong that MacNeil received death threats. The Montreal police took the threats seriously and provided him with around-the-clock protection.

"They were with me 24 hours on the hop for seven days," MacNeil told the *Calgary Herald's* Al Maki three decades after the incident. "I had a police officer right on the bench with me. I was going to ask him if he could help me on the power play."

While MacNeil could joke about the controversy, he said he got angry because it bothered his wife Norma.

The Richard incident didn't affect MacNeil's coaching decisions. Instead of holding a grudge, he put Richard back in the lineup, and the Pocket Rocket responded with two key goals to give Montreal a 3–2 win in Game 7. With a capacity crowd hanging from the rafters in Chicago Stadium, the Blackhawks took a 2–0 lead. Jacques Lemaire put the Canadiens on the board, and then Richard supplied the tying goal and the Cup-winner early in the third period.

While Richard scored the key goals, it was Dryden who sealed the win when he stopped Jim Pappin with 10 minutes to play. Pappin was on the doorstep of the Montreal crease when he redirected a perfect pass into what appeared to be an open net. Pappin was so sure he had scored the tying goal that he raised his stick in celebration. But Dryden managed to get his right pad on the puck.

That save was probably the deciding factor in Dryden being named the winner of the Conn Smythe Trophy, which goes to the most valuable player in the playoffs. The following season, Dryden won the Calder Trophy as the NHL's top rookie, and, to this day, he's the only player to be named rookie of the year after winning the Conn Smythe Trophy.

MacNeil's problems weren't limited to French-Canadian players. John Ferguson wasn't happy when he lost playing time to young American Bobby Sheehan. But it was the language question that hung over MacNeil's future with the team.

MacNeil and Richard hugged after the victory, and MacNeil was carried around the ice on the shoulders of two French-Canadian players—Pierre Bouchard and Marc Tardif. But it was obvious that MacNeil was in a difficult position. He took a short vacation, and, when he returned, he told General Manger Sam Pollock that he couldn't continue as the coach.

The Canadiens had decided to move the Voyageurs to Halifax, and the team announced that MacNeil, a Nova Scotia native, was being "promoted" to general manager and coach of the Nova Scotia Voyageurs. In his first season in Nova Scotia, the world's worst coach led the Voyageurs to a Calder Cup title.

He got his name on the Stanley Cup two more times as the Canadiens' director of player personnel in 1978 and 1979.

Looking back on the tumultuous Stanley Cup season 30 years later, MacNeil said: "I remember telling Ted Blackman, who worked for the *Montreal Gazette*, 'I've been called lots of things by my mother that were worse than what Richard had said.' Winning that Cup was probably the most satisfying thing that happened. It wasn't a fun thing so much as satisfying."

Out of His Element

Teams travel exclusively by charter today, but on November 27, 1995, the Canadiens were sitting in the departure lounge of the Montreal airport awaiting a commercial flight to Detroit.

They were scheduled to leave at 12:45 PM, but the Northwest Airlines aircraft was still in Detroit experiencing delays because of fog and post-Thanksgiving traffic.

There was a buzz about the trip because Mario Tremblay, the Canadiens' rookie coach, would be facing coaching legend Scotty Bowman for the first time. Tremblay collected five Stanley Cup rings during his playing career, and Bowman was behind the bench for four of those victories. As we waited for the flight, Tremblay talked about the influence Bowman had on his career.

"I think the most important thing I learned from Scotty was the importance of a well-organized practice," Tremblay said. "He used to say that one hour was the perfect time for a practice if you concentrated and worked hard. And he was a master behind the bench. It seemed that he always knew the right move to make."

But you got the idea that the relationship between Bowman the coach and Tremblay the player wasn't always a happy one. Tremblay said he almost quit in his second and third seasons with the Canadiens because Bowman was constantly riding him, telling that he couldn't skate or that he couldn't shoot.

When Tremblay took over as coach of the Canadiens, he acknowledged his link to Bowman and called him one of the greatest coaches ever. But he also said he didn't want to be like Bowman. He recalled Bowman's habit of keeping his players on edge by not telling them until the last minute whether they would be dressed for a game. "Sometimes, you would show up at the rink and learn that you weren't playing because there was no sweater in your locker."

When Bowman was asked about Tremblay's comments, he said that he could accept criticism of his coaching style, but he did admit one regret.

"I just wish I could have told those guys how good they were," said Bowman.

Tremblay is best remembered for his second meeting against Bowman. Four days after dropping a 3–2 decision to the Red Wings in Detroit, the Canadiens absorbed an 11–1 loss at the Montreal Forum. Tremblay left goaltender Patrick Roy in net for nine of those goals, and when he was finally replaced, Roy confronted team president Ronald Corey and said he had played his last game for the Canadiens.

The situation with Roy might have been avoided except that a little too much of Bowman had rubbed off on Tremblay. It also might have helped if Tremblay came into the coaching job with some experience. Tremblay was a surprise choice to coach the team when Corey decided to clean house after the Canadiens opened the 1995–96 season with four losses. General Manager Serge Savard and head coach Jacques Demers were the major casualties, and new general manager Réjean Houle hired former teammate Tremblay as his coach.

At the time, Tremblay was working as a broadcaster, and one of his favorite themes was the way Demers handled Roy. He accused Demers of coddling the goaltender. Tremblay and Roy exchanged angry words in a hotel coffee shop before the Canadiens game in Long Island on October 21. What Roy didn't know at the time was that Tremblay had been offered the head coaching job and would be introduced as Demers' successor a day later.

Roy wasn't the only player who clashed with Tremblay. In his second season, he got into a shouting match with tough guy Donald Brashear, an altercation which led to Brashear being traded to Vancouver. Skilled players like Pierre Turgeon and Brian Savage felt that their talents weren't appreciated.

Tremblay made the playoffs in both of his two seasons behind the bench, but he resigned after the 1996–97 season and blamed the media for his decision, saying: "A coach has to live with criticism, but there's a point where it has to stop. When they do things to try and break you, that's not right."

In the end, Tremblay was done in by his lack of experience.

It was something Jacques Lemaire touched on a few days before he led the New Jersey Devils to a five-game round win over the Canadiens in the first-round of the 1997 playoffs.

Said Lemaire: "We all learned the same system, we all know how the game should be played. The difference is in how you teach that system."

Teaching isn't something you learn overnight. There are few natural teachers, and Tremblay's greatest failure as a coach was his inability to understand that.

Houle made the initial mistake when he hastily drew up the job description for the Canadiens coaching position after he succeeded Savard and specified no experience necessary.

And Tremblay compounded that mistake when he accepted a job for which he wasn't prepared. This was a case of extreme hubris on Tremblay's part. He wanted to coach the Canadiens, but he didn't believe he had to pay his dues. He had previously turned down coaching opportunities at the junior level, in the American Hockey League, and as an assistant in the National Hockey League. Any of those jobs would have served one of two purposes: They would have given him an understanding of what's involved in coaching and provided him with the experience needed.

Or they might have proved to Tremblay, or others, that he wasn't suited to be a coach.

That's the way every other team in the NHL does things. The other coaches in the NHL came to the job with previous experience as a head coach or assistant in the NHL, or as a head coach at the junior, college, or minor level. That's not to say there couldn't be an exception to the rule. There could be, but Tremblay wasn't it.

After his first season, Tremblay was encouraged to attend Roger Neilson's annual summer coaching clinic. This was an opportunity for coaches from all levels from the NHL down to minor hockey to exchange ideas, but Tremblay felt this was beneath him.

Tremblay was given a chance to play in the NHL at age 18, but he had little use for young players. He kept Craig Rivet and David Wilkie with the NHL club, but used them sparingly. He talked about playing 19-year-old Terry Ryan in 35–40 games to get him the experience he needed. Ryan played only a handful of shifts and was going nowhere when a concussion sidetracked his NHL career.

Tremblay started his second season with the youngest team in the NHL, but it became progressively older as the season went on. The veteran additions—guys like Shayne Corson, Stéphane Richer, Jassen Cullimore, Scott Thornton, and Dave Manson— were supposed to be the difference in the playoffs. In some respects they were. Thornton stood out and Corson worked hard, but Richer didn't show up, Manson was a liability because he took some stupid penalties, and Cullimore watched the end of the series from the press box.

Tremblay never understood that part of a coach's job is to make sure his team is ready to play. The Canadiens surrendered the first goal in 43 of their 82 games. Tremblay dismissed the importance of shots on goal and talked about scoring chances, but shots do reflect whether a team is playing good defense and the Canadiens were outshot 50 times. And then there was the Canadiens' sorry record for penalty-killing. This is an area in which coaching and hard work go hand in hand, but the Canadiens ranked last in the league all season and were even worse in the playoffs. It was no surprise in the postseason that they were victimized by a New Jersey power play that was one of the worst in the NHL.

When Tremblay resigned, he left the impression that he was driven from the game by cruel attacks from the media. "I did my job with passion," he said. "In terms of hockey, it was great."

Nobody can doubt that Tremblay had passion and that he worked hard. But mostly, the work was unproductive. In terms of hockey, it wasn't great; it was barely mediocre. The Canadiens finished the season five games below .500. Sure, there were injuries that crippled the team, but the Canadiens went into the playoffs with a healthy lineup, and only an inspired overtime win in Game 4 prevented a New Jersey sweep.

Tremblay never held another head coaching position, but he did spend nine seasons as an assistant coach under Lemaire in Minnesota. He also accompanied Lemaire when he returned to the Devils in 2009. When Lemaire retired in 2010, Tremblay wasn't rehired as an assistant coach, and he returned to Montreal as a broadcaster with RDS.

The Reluctant Coach

When Jacques Lemaire's Hall of Fame playing career ended, he went to France and coached La Serre in the low-key French League. At the time, he said he always wanted to try his hand at coaching, and he described the job as an adventure.

When he returned to North America, he spent one season as an assistant coach at Plattsburgh State College, a Division III school 90 minutes south of Montreal.

Neither of those experiences prepared him for stepping into one of the most pressurized jobs in the National Hockey League, coaching the Canadiens.

It was a job he never wanted, and he walked away from it after his first full season on the job.

The announcement was made at a hastily called afternoon news conference at the Forum in late July 1985. The news came as a surprise to some, but veteran writer Red Fisher said it shouldn't have been because Lemaire never wanted the job.

"When they asked me to take over at the end of the 1983–84 season [when Bob Berry was fired with 17 games to go], I knew the team was at its lowest point, and I felt I could help the team," explained Lemaire. "I said I'd take the job, but only to the end of the season."

Lemaire was persuaded to remain in the job through the 1984–85 season, while Jean Perron served his professional apprenticeship as an assistant coach. Jacques Laperriere, also an assistant coach with the Habs, had never shown any interest in the top job.

"Up until last week I hoped Jacques [Lemaire] would change his mind and stay on in order to give Perron another year's experience, but he wouldn't," said General Manager Serge Savard. "As director of personnel he'll be working with all the coaches in our system as well as doing some advance scouting, and that's exactly the job he wants to do."

Lemaire never made it past the Wales Conference Final in his two years, though reaching the conference final against the Islanders in his rookie year was considered a major achievement. The next year, the Canadiens finished first in the Adams Division and eliminated the Boston Bruins in the first round of the play-offs before bowing to the Quebec Nordiques in a hard-fought seven-game division final. Lemaire's playoff mark was 15–12. In his one full season and 17 games, Lemaire piloted the Habs to a 48–37–12 won-lost-tied record.

"Every coach would like to win the Stanley Cup," Lemaire conceded, "but you've got to go with your own life. In life you have to do something you like and feel good about and enjoy. When I went home to relax, whether we won or lost, I couldn't relax, I kept thinking about what I should do to win the next game. I'm not saying it's too much pressure. It's just a thing I don't want to do."

The decision caught some players by surprise.

"I had no inkling," said veteran defenseman Larry Robinson, who played with Lemaire in the 1970s. "But knowing Jacques the way I do, I suppose that's not unusual. Jacques is very good at keeping things to himself."

Montreal captain Bob Gainey, another former teammate of Lemaire, said the timing of the announcement was a little unexpected, but not entirely shocking.

"Everybody knew when he took over the team it wasn't his idea," Gainey said. "He had to be convinced to do it. Jacques never looked at this as a long-term thing."

Canadiens president Ronald Corey said he had hoped Lemaire would "enjoy the job for five or 10 years." But he admitted that "Jacques always said he didn't want to coach, and you can't force a guy to do a job he doesn't want to do."

Somewhere along the line, Lemaire decided he did want to coach as long as he didn't have to deal with the pressure that went along with the job in Montreal. In 1993, he signed on with the New Jersey Devils, and, a season later, he guided the team to a Stanley Cup in the strike-shortened 1994–95 season.

My favorite memory of Lemaire came from the Canadiens' visit to what was then known as the Brendan Byrne Arena located on reclaimed swampland in the Meadowlands.

It was the 18th game of the season for the Devils, and they were fighting for a playoff spot with a 6–7–4 record. Upon arriving for the morning skate, I ran into Claude Lemieux, the veteran forward whose career began in Montreal when Lemaire was coaching the Canadiens.

When I asked Lemieux how things were going, he unleashed a string of profanities directed at Lemaire.

"Coco hasn't given us a day off since the season started," said Lemieux. "It takes all the energy I have to keep Stéphane [Richer] from killing him."

When I talked to Lemaire, he admitted that he had been pushing his team hard, but he set the record straight. He said the Devils had been off the ice for one day since the season officially opened on January 14. He pointed out that he had planned to give the players a break the previous day, but he changed his mind after the Devils tied the Washington Capitals 3–3.

"They know the reason they are not getting a day off is because I am not satisfied with the way they played," Lemaire said. "One thing I know—if they want a day off, it will be easy for them to get it. They just have to play well. If I am a player and I want a day off, and all I have to do is play well to earn it, I'd try to play well. It's not so difficult."

That night, Lemieux had one goal and one assist, and the Devils crushed the Canadiens 6–1. When I wrote my early lead, I was confident that this game qualified as playing well, and I suggested that the Devils would be getting their over-due day off.

When I finished my interviews in the Canadiens dressing room, I crossed the hall to the Devils' room. When I spotted Lemieux, I said: "I guess you'll enjoy the day off."

"Yeah, look at that," he said as he pointed to a bulletin board that read: "Practice tomorrow, 4:00 PM."

I quickly returned to the press box to rewrite my story.

It took another five days and a 6–1 win over Florida for the Devils to get their day off, but Lemaire must have been doing something right because the Devils won the Stanley Cup that season, sweeping the favored Detroit Red Wings in the final.

The Old College Try

On May 14, 1988, Jean Perron returned to Montreal after a vacation in Guadeloupe. He was greeted by reporters who wanted to know about his status with the Canadiens. His three-year contract to coach the club was expiring on June 30, and there was speculation that he wouldn't get a new deal.

The Canadiens finished the regular season with the second-best regular-season record in the NHL but had been bounced by Boston in the second round of the playoffs. Future Hall of Famer Larry Robinson, Claude Lemieux, and Chris Nilan openly criticized the coach, and there were whispers that Perron had lost the room.

That's the kiss of death for a coach, and after a three-hour meeting with General Manager Serge Savard to discuss the team, the Canadiens announced that Perron had resigned "for family reasons." The announcement came 36 hours after Perron said: "I've never quit."

Perron guided the Canadiens to a Stanley Cup in 1986, his first season as a professional head coach. But he had trouble winning the respect of players who saw him as an outsider, the college boy who had no business coaching in the NHL. The players' contempt for Perron was reflected in their nickname for him— Puddin' Head.

He had trouble maintaining discipline. The Canadiens were sequestered before the first-round playoff series against Hartford, but three players—Shayne Corson, Petr Svoboda, and Chris Chelios—managed to skip out. Their absence might have gone undetected if they hadn't been involved in a minor car accident.

During a West Coast trip, Perron caught one of his players breaking curfew not once, but twice, on the same night. Savard called Perron in and said he had to crack down on discipline. But during the talk, Perron complained his boss only talked to him about negative things.

Savard had backed the coach in January when Nilan, the team's veteran enforcer, launched an obscenity-laden verbal assault at the coach prior to a practice and later flipped a puck that caught Perron in the face.

"Jean was going around the room and telling everyone what they could be doing better," recalled Nilan. "When he got to me, he said: 'Chris Nilan, when was the last time you had a fight?' I never had a coach tell me to fight; I never needed a coach to tell me when to fight. Here's this guy who's never had a fight in his life, and he's talking to me about fighting.

"I lost it and I told him what he could do and he went crying to Serge," said Nilan, "Serge told me there are things you just can't do, but I had had enough of the guy."

Nilan, a nine-year veteran, was upset because Perron had cut his ice time by taking him off a line with Bob Gainey and Guy Carbonneau.

"He didn't have a clue," said Nilan. "We'd practice and he'd have us doing these stupid drills he used in college. The guys ignored him. [Captain Bob] Gainey and Larry [Robinson] ran the show."

Nilan said he had been thinking about asking for a trade, but Savard beat him to the punch. The GM had enough respect for Nilan that he asked him where he wanted to go. Nilan's first choice was to go home to Boston, but Savard nixed that idea and made a deal to send Nilan to the New York Rangers.

"[The trade] shattered me," said Nilan. "I don't know how guys like Bobby Dollas and Brent Ashton, guys who were traded a lot, handled it. I played for two other teams and it was tough."

A little bit of trivia: The 1988 deal that sent Chris Nilan to the New York Rangers gave Montreal the higher of the teams' first-round draft picks in 1989. The Canadiens went to the Stanley Cup Final that year and would have picked 20th, but they took the Rangers' spot at No. 13. The move didn't work out because they selected Lindsay Vallis, who would play one game in the NHL. The Rangers selected Steven Rice. He played 11 of his 329 NHL games with the Rangers but was part of the 1991 deal that brought Mark Messier and Jeff Beukeboom from Edmonton to New York.

Larry Robinson criticized Perron's use of his players, saying that several players—he named Kjell Dahlin and Sergio Momesso—deserved more ice time. Robinson also felt he should play more. Robinson's outburst resulted in Robinson, Dahlin, and Momesso suddenly getting more ice time.

"I didn't mind him because he played me a lot, and I got time on the power play, but he did a lot of strange things," said Momesso, who currently serves as an analyst on the Canadiens radio broadcasts.

Robinson offered some grudging praise for the coach when the Canadiens went undefeated in 12 games late in the season: "I guess he must be doing something right. A team can't go 12 games without a loss by itself...can it?"

Claude Lemieux questioned Perron's authority late in the season, confronting Perron between periods of a game at the Forum over his lack of ice time. Perron sent Lemieux home. The initial report said Lemieux was suspended indefinitely, but Savard reduced the sentence to one game.

Robinson said he wasn't surprised that Perron quit and added: "If he's resigning because of the pressure, he shouldn't have taken the job in the first place."

So how did Perron get one of the choicest jobs in hockey? It was a matter of being in the right place at the right time.

He was 37 and largely unknown outside the world of Canadian university hockey when he was hired as an assistant coach under Jacques Lemaire in 1984. Savard and team president Ronald Corey were impressed by the young man who had come highly recommended by former general manager Sam Pollock. The idea was to groom him as a possible replacement for Lemaire, and the timetable was moved up after Lemaire abruptly quit after only one full season behind the bench.

Savard admitted the changeover was a year ahead of schedule, but when Lemaire assured him and Corey, "I would have coached [another year] if I didn't think Jean was ready," the time became now.

Perron's story was a rags-to-riches saga worthy of Horatio Alger.

He started off in rural Quebec with a pair of mismatched skates in a dirt-poor family of 10.

His story is stereotypical of the thousands of Quebec youngsters who grew up idolizing the Canadiens and dreaming of being the next Rocket Richard, Jean Béliveau, or Doug Harvey. They were the kids who learned to skate in hand-me-down equipment on outdoor rinks.

Perron was the third of eight children—four boys and four girls—born to André and Antoinette Perron. When Jean was three, the family moved to Ascot Corner, seven miles east of Sherbrooke.

"We were very, very poor. There were a lot of fights in the family about money," Perron recalled when he was hired. "My first skates really didn't match, and I used to take the long way to the rink so no one would see them. When I lost one of the blades, I got a used pair that did match for $5. My mother used to give us a piece of equipment at Christmas when she could afford it."

"My dad was tough, and he thought sports were a waste of time. My mother used to tell us to hide our hockey stuff in the shed so dad wouldn't see it. When we'd sneak out of the house on Saturday mornings and play all day, my dad would go out of his mind."

Education seemed the only escape from poverty and also the best way to pursue his love of sports. A parochial school run by the Capuchin Fathers, 130 miles away in Cap Rouge near Quebec City, fit the bill.

The only way he could manage the cost was on a learn-now, pay-later plan. It was the same thing throughout the 11 years he spent in school, first at Cap Rouge, a Sherbrooke classical seminary, and then the University of Sherbrooke, and finally a year at Michigan State, where he earned his master's degree in physical education. He went in hock for a total of $15,000.

Perron could have taken an easier route when he was ready for university. St. Lawrence University offered him a four-year, full-ride athletic scholarship to bring his hockey talents to the upstate New York private school, but he opted for the University of Sherbrooke.

"There wasn't much future for a university player from our team then," Perron said. "Three of us could have played in the International League, but they were only offering $5,000 a year, and I knew I could start teaching at $6,000. I guess that's where I set my path on coaching."

Three years at College Matane—"They had great sports facilities there"—and Perron was faced with another decision: Accept a city recreation director's job for $12,000 a year or go back to school and get his master's degree. He wisely chose the latter and went on to Michigan State, where he helped coach the Spartans' junior varsity hockey team as part of his internship.

The extra degree proved to be the ticket he needed to land his first major coaching job, at a starting salary of $11,000, the same as he was making in Matane. Athletic director Vance Toner was looking for a new hockey coach for his University of Moncton Blue Eagles. It was the beginning a successful and happy 10-year marriage. Perron's teams won four conference titles and back-to-back Canadian university championships (1981–82).

"We wanted an educator-coach, and he delivered exactly that," added Toner. "Probably what impressed me the most over the years was his concern for his players' education. In 10 years, only two of his players failed to graduate with a degree. He was really true to our philosophy."

That's when Sam Pollock stepped in. He pursued a number of business ventures after stepping down as the Canadiens GM in 1979, but he stayed involved with the amateur hockey establishment. These were the days when Canada went into Olympic competition with amateur players. Pollock championed Father David Bauer's idea of bringing together young players in a centralized national team. In the run up to the 1984 Winter Games, he turned to Dave King from the University of Saskatchewan to coach the team with Perron as his No. 1 assistant.

Pollock was impressed with the rapport between Perron and the players on the national team. Knowing the importance of finding French-speaking coaches for the Canadiens organization, he suggested that Savard hire Perron.

Perron accepted the Canadiens job offer with some reluctance.

"It wasn't a case of not wanting to," Perron said, "but back then we all had an inferiority complex, and we didn't think we were good enough because the Canadiens seemed to have a history of not hiring French Canadians as a head coach. There was 'Piton' (Claude Ruel, who coached them twice), but that was mainly a transitional thing."

The Canadiens' job turned out to be transitional for Perron. His success with young players never translated to the professional level. After the Canadiens let him go, Perron had only one other shot at an NHL job. He signed on as assistant GM of the Quebec Nordiques after the Canadiens let him go. When Ron Lapointe was diagnosed with cancer, Perron moved behind the bench but was relieved of his duties at the end of the season. He had a 16–25–5 record with the Nordiques.

Lame Duck from the Start

There's an adage in sports that says the day a coach is hired is the first step on the road to being fired.

It didn't take long for Randy Cunneyworth to realize the truth of that statement.

Cunneyworth was 50 years old when he was named interim coach of the Canadiens on December 17, 2011. But two days after he replaced Jacques Martin, it became painfully obvious that

Cunneyworth would never be hired permanently for the head coaching job.

It had little to do with his coaching ability, although Cunneyworth might have had more of a case for keeping the job if he hadn't finished the season with a 18–23–9 record.

Cunneyworth was doomed because he couldn't speak French. The reaction to his hiring among Quebec's French-speaking population was mostly negative. Christine St-Pierre, Quebec's culture minister, called on team owner Geoff Molson to rectify the situation as soon as possible. Nationalist groups called for a boycott of Molson beer, and there were protesters outside the Bell Centre before Cunneyworth's first game against the New Jersey Devils.

The French-language media criticized the hiring, although there was little sympathy for Martin. Several media outlets promoted the idea of bringing in former Canadiens goaltender Patrick Roy, who was enjoying some success as the coach of the Quebec Remparts junior team.

The heat was so intense that Molson issued a statement two days after Cunneyworth was hired, and he made it clear that Cunneyworth would be replaced at the end of the season and the new coach would speak French.

"On Saturday, our general manager Pierre Gauthier made a coaching change and named Randy Cunneyworth interim head coach of the Montreal Canadiens until the end of the 2011–12 season," Molson said in the statement. "This important decision was made with the objective of giving the team a much-needed spark after disappointing results since the start of the 2011–12 season. We are responsible for providing our fans and partners with a winning team and believe that this move will contribute to improving the overall performance of our team and produce positive results this season. The action was taken to remedy the situation without further delay.

"Randy Cunneyworth is a qualified and experienced coach who has earned the respect of the players and everyone within the organization, and he was ready to take over the responsibility of head coach," Molson said. "As Pierre Gauthier indicated, the head coaching position will be evaluated at the end of the season, and at that time the selection process will be carefully planned. Although our main priority remains to win hockey games and to keep improving as a team, it is obvious that the ability for the head coach to express himself in both French and English will be a very important factor in the selection of the permanent head coach."

The Canadiens had come into the season with high expectations. Gauthier had added free agent winger Erik Cole, Max Pacioretty had recovered from the injuries he suffered when he was run into a stanchion by Boston's Zdeno Chara, and Carey Price was coming off a bounce-back season after the Canadiens showed their confidence in him by trading Jaroslav Halak.

When Montreal lost seven of its first eight games, Gauthier sent a message to Martin by firing Perry Pearn, who was both Martin's top assistant and longtime friend.

Pearn left town without speaking, but a week after his departure, he was interviewed on television and suggested that he was being made a scapegoat for the slow start.

"I'm a proud person—I think I'm good at what I do, so I can't help but be disappointed that what's happened has happened," he said. "Do I think it's my fault the Montreal Canadiens had a bad start? I'll take my share of the responsibility. Our power play wasn't as good as it should be; our penalty-killing wasn't as good as we wanted it to be. But to say I'm the only reason we had a bad start—no, I don't accept that.

"And I'm sure that's not the point of me being let go, is that it was all my fault. It was a way of sending a wake-up call to everybody that things had to change.

"I had two good years here, successful years given the competitive nature of our team in the playoffs," Pearn added. "I'm not hanging my head in shame by any stretch of the imagination. I do think I've had a positive impact in lots of areas, in terms of helping the team become a little bit better than it was the day we arrived."

Martin also was a bit of a scapegoat. After the slow start, the Canadiens had a 13–12–7 record when Martin was fired. Two days earlier, the Canadiens lost 4–3 to Philadelphia, but they had gone 3–0–2 in their five previous games.

Nothing went right after Cunneyworth took over. Captain Brian Gionta was sidelined by a biceps injury; Michael Cammalleri was traded in the middle of a game; Cammalleri's replacement, René Bourque, was a dud; and Scott Gomez was making north of $7 million but couldn't buy a goal.

Gauthier didn't last the season. He was relieved of his duties on March 29, and Cunneyworth was left in limbo. When Marc Bergevin was named general manager on May 2, he announced that Cunneyworth's days as head coach were over, but he would remain with the team as an assistant coach. But shortly after Michel Therrien was hired as the head coach on June 1, he announced that Cunneyworth and Assistant Coach Randy Ladouceur had both been fired.

Déjà Vu All Over Again

Claude Julien and his family were enjoying a winter vacation in rural Vermont when the phone rang. It was Canadiens general manager Marc Bergevin, and he wanted to know whether Julien was interested in returning to coach the Canadiens.

It had been less than a week since Julien had been fired by the Boston Bruins after a couple of seasons swinging in the wind. The call came as a surprise. The Canadiens were in a bye week, and Coach Michel Therrien had them in a position to finish first in the Atlantic Division.

But there were signs of trouble in Montreal. The Canadiens had lost six of their eight games heading into the break, and

Claude Julien instructs his team during the third period of a 2017 game against the Calgary Flames. *(Todd Korol/The Canadian Press via AP)*

Bergevin felt the need to replace Therrien, the coach he had hired in 2012, the coach he had described as his foxhole buddy. The decision was made easier because Julien was available.

"I told Marc honestly that when I was let go by the Bruins, I really felt like I should maybe sit back and let the season finish," Julien said. "That was my initial thought. Obviously, it happened quickly."

It's difficult to turn down a five-year contact worth $5 million a season. Julien said he would take the job, bringing his coaching career full circle. The Canadiens gave him his first NHL coaching gig on January 17, 2003, when he was promoted from the AHL Hamilton Bulldogs to replace Therrien.

It was disappointing to see Therrien go. After a disastrous 2015–16 campaign when goaltender Carey Price missed most of the season with a knee injury, the Canadiens has returned to form. But there was reason for concern when they headed into the bye on a four-game losing streak. They were shut out in the two games preceding the break, and it appeared that a number of players, including Price, had quit on Therrien.

At the same time, you had to feel happy for Julien, who was returning to Montreal with a five-year contract. Julien is the kind of guy you would like to sit down and talk to over a beer. My colleague Stu Cowan said Julien reminded him of a favorite uncle.

But no coach of Julien's caliber has been treated as badly as Julien, and that, too, started in Montreal.

Julien was hired by André Savard as a midseason replacement in 2003, but, five months later, Savard was fired and replaced by Bob Gainey. A change at the top is never a good thing for a coach because general managers like to hire their own people, and, three years into Julien's tenure, Gainey decided that his guy was former teammate Guy Carbonneau, who was working in the Dallas Stars front office. Carbonneau's coaching experience was limited to two seasons as an assistant coach under Therrien, and Gainey decided to ease him into the job. Gainey installed himself as head coach and gave Carbonneau the title of associate coach with the understanding he would move into the top job the following season.

The Canadiens had a 19–16–6 record when Julien was fired, and he had a credible winning percentage of .542 in his three seasons behind the bench.

Julien didn't have to wait long for his next job. Lou Lamoriello hired him to coach the New Jersey Devils on June 13, 2006, and he had the team in first place with a 47–24–8 record when he was suddenly fired with three games remaining in the regular season. Lamoriello, who assumed the coaching duties, said he made the move because he didn't feel Julien had the team ready for the playoffs.

The situation was more complicated than that.

The Devils' success had been built on the goaltending of Martin Brodeur and a trapping defense that smothered the opposition. New Jersey had the most boring team in the NHL, but it didn't matter because the Devils were winning.

Julien looked at his roster and felt he could get more out of talented offensive players like Patrik Elias, Zach Parise, Scott Gomez, and Brian Gionta if the Devils opened things up a bit. This idea did not go over well with Brodeur and some of the veterans, who felt that the coach was robbing the Devils of their identity. Brodeur, in particular, was concerned that a change in style would have an adverse effect on his statistics.

Again, Julien did not have to wait long for a new job. The Boston Bruins hired him, and he was able to test his theory that it was possible to play good hockey at both ends of the ice. In the 2008–09 season, the Bruins had the best goals against average in the league at 2.32, and they were No. 2 in scoring behind the Detroit Red Wings.

Under Julien, the Bruins had gone from a team that missed the playoffs in the two years prior to his hiring to a Cup contender, but storm clouds were gathering. Cam Neely, a Hall of Fame winger with the Bruins, rejoined the team as executive vice president in 2007 and was named president three years later. As Neely assumed more power, that thing about wanting his own people started taking form. He seemed determined to dump Julien and General Manager Peter Chiarelli.

"We were gone, and then we won the Cup," Chiarelli told me after an exhibition game a few months after the Bruins won the 2011 Stanley Cup by upsetting the Vancouver Canucks in seven games. "It's hard to fire people after you've won the Cup."

The Bruins made a return visit to the Stanley Cup Final in 2013, and Carey Price and the Canadiens ended their 2014 run. But the Bruins missed the playoffs in 2015. Chiarelli was fired and went off to Edmonton in time to draft Connor McDavid.

After missing the playoffs a second time in 2016, it seemed only a matter of time before Julien would pay the price. He was fired on February 7, 2017, one game shy of coaching his 1,000th NHL game.

Julien went into the 2017–18 season with a points percentage of .605, which puts him among the NHL elite—Toronto's Mike Babcock was at .609.

While it can be argued that no successful coach has endured such abuse in his career, Julien doesn't hold any grudges.

"There are only 31 coaching jobs in the NHL, and I've been fortunate to have one of them for a long time," said Julien.

CHAPTER 13
HABS BEHAVING BADLY

There's a tendency to place athletes on a pedestal, to hold them up as role models.

There are some athletes who fall into this category. I've never met a finer gentleman than Jean Béliveau. Ken Dryden walked away from a successful career and devoted himself to public service. Doug Jarvis leads a life guided by his Christian principles without being preachy.

But when NBA star Charles Barkley was asked whether he felt it was important for athletes to be role models, he made it clear that it was a responsibility he wasn't prepared to accept.

"I'm not a role model.... Just because I dunk a basketball doesn't mean I should raise your kids."

Athletes are human, and, on occasion, they make mistakes that hurt them and others. Here's a look at some Canadiens who stepped over the line.

Zack, We Hardly Knew You

General Manager Marc Bergevin's quest to add some size and grit to the lineup led him to Zack Kassian in the summer of 2015.

At 6 foot 3 and 217 pounds, Kassian was the quintessential power forward. In addition to his size, Bergevin was attracted to Kassian because he was a right winger and because he had a mean streak. He also came with a history, and that's why there were some raised eyebrows when Bergevin kicked off his July 1 activities by trading the popular Brandon Prust to Vancouver and receiving Kassian in return.

There was no questioning Kassian's potential. He was a first-round draft choice of the Buffalo Sabres in 2009, and he had led the Windsor Spitfires to the Memorial Cup in 2010.

But Kassian had problems off the ice. Shortly after the Memorial Cup win, Kassian was charged with assault after a fight in a Windsor bar. A conviction could have resulted in a ban on travel to the United States, effectively ending his dream of an NHL career. Kassian got lucky when the prosecutor dropped the charges after Kassian agreed to do 25 hours of community service, donate $500 to charity, and pay for the victim's dental work.

Kassian made his NHL debut with the Sabres in 2010, but things did not go well in Buffalo. He was traded to Vancouver for Cody Hodgson, another rookie whose performance fell short of expectations.

Kassian scored 14 goals in his first full season with the Canucks, but his career went off the rails in the 2014–15 season. There was a suspension for a high stick, which broke the jaw of Edmonton's Sam Gagner. There were some injuries, and there was an enforced absence as he went through stage one of the NHL's substance abuse program.

Bergevin was aware of Kassian's problems with alcohol, and he made it clear to the player that he would be on a short leash. "It's strike one and you're out," Bergevin told Kassian.

Kassian reported to training camp in excellent shape, and coach Michel Therrien was delighted with his play in exhibition games. Kassian was penciled in as the right winger on the third line, but Therrien noted that he had skill that would enable him to move up if the Canadiens ran into injuries.

But Kassian's fortunes changed in the early morning hours on October 4. It was shortly after 6:00 AM, when a Ford F-350 truck driven by a 20-year-old woman jumped the curb and ran into a tree in Notre Dame de Grace, a quiet residential neighborhood west of the downtown core. The driver and an 18-year-old woman in the passenger seat suffered minor injuries. Kassian, who was sitting in the rear seat, suffered a broken nose and a broken foot.

Kassian identified himself to a man who lived across the street from the crash scene, and it didn't take long for the story to spread through social media.

Bergevin felt a sense of betrayal as he addressed reporters the day after the accident.

"I do not have all the information, but it is disappointing to say the least," said Bergevin, who was notified of the accident that morning by the team doctor. "You have to be respectful. You're lucky to be hockey players.

"I'm a firm believer in character, and that's really a lack of character and judgment on his part."

When Bergevin did get all the information, Kassian was suspended without pay and entered stage two of the NHL substance abuse program. He went through a two-month residential program in southern California. When Kassian completed the program, he returned to Montreal, but the Canadiens made it clear that his career in Montreal was over.

On December 28, he was traded to the Edmonton Oilers for goaltender Ben Scrivens.

The Kassian story has had a happy ending.

"The best thing for my career was the car accident to be honest," Kassian told reporters when he returned to Montreal two months after the trade. "It was an eye-opener. Who knows what would have happened if that car accident never happened? At the time it's tough to swallow, but over the last four months I've learned to be okay with it and just move on. I'm just looking to build up my reputation again."

Kassian said he didn't harbor any ill feelings toward the Canadiens.

"They were great to me when I was here," he said. "Marc's a great person, the team, a bunch of great guys. I couldn't thank the team enough. Obviously what happened to me was negative, but at the same time what came from that was me finally realizing that I needed help, and I got it and now it's just a matter of me staying on top of it. Now I have an opportunity to play for the Edmonton Oilers, and I'm very thankful for that. I'm not mad at Montreal by any means. If anything I'm mad at myself for screwing up that opportunity."

Kassian had to sell himself to his new teammates and the fans who remembered the hit on Gagner, but his hard work and his willingness to stand up for his teammates won them over. He was a solid contributor in the 2016–17 season as the Oilers returned to the playoffs for the first time since 2006. His three playoff goals included two game-winning goals.

Two Wild and Crazy Guys

The Canadiens are on the road at Christmas time each year, and players often grab a few extra days in Florida before playing post-Christmas games in Tampa and Sunrise. That was the case in 2007 when the Canadiens played in Dallas on December 23 and a half-dozen players went directly to Florida.

I was sitting in the lobby of the Tampa Marriott Waterside hotel on December 26 when brothers Andrei and Sergei Kostitsyn arrived after a few days on South Beach.

The Thrashers' Eric Perrin get caught in between brothers Andrei (left) and Sergei Kostitsyn. (AP Photo/The Canadian Press, Paul Chiasson)

The first thing that struck me was their resemblance to the Festrunk brothers. Fans of vintage *Saturday Night Live* will recall the characters Georg and Yortuk Festrunk as portrayed by Dan Aykroyd and Steve Martin. They were Czech immigrants, self-styled wild and crazy guys who spent their time unsuccessfully trying to pick up women with fractured English laced with double entendre.

The Kostitsyns could have doubled for the Festrunks with their bad haircuts, too tight pants, and wild patterned sport shirts unbuttoned to showcase their chest hair. On the ice, the brothers were talented, but, by the time they left North America, there was the feeling that NHL fans never saw their best hockey.

Andrei was drafted 10th overall in 2003, and the Canadiens felt they had achieved a coup in landing the Belarusian. Nobody questioned Kostitsyn's talent, but most teams were scared off by his medical history. He suffered a number of seizures, and there were suggestions that his health problems may been the result of growing up downwind from the Chernobyl power plant that was the site of a nuclear accident in 1986.

Dr. David Mulder, the Canadiens' team physician, was tasked with exploring Kostitsyn's medical records. He found some deficiencies in the player's diet and also recommended a change in his medication. Kostitsyn's health improved almost immediately, but he had a scare when he arrived for the Canadiens development camp in 2004. He suffered a seizure, but Mulder said a combination of jet lag and a failure to take his medication led to the seizure. He didn't suffer any other problems during his career.

Andrei had only two seasons when he lived up to his first-round billing. He had 26 goals in the 2007–08 season and 23 goals the following year playing on a line with Tomas Plekanec and Alex Kovalev. His numbers dipped after Kovalev left for Ottawa in 2009.

Sergei Kostitsyn was drafted in the seventh round in 2005, but he rose to prominence after joining the London Knights junior team. He finished third in the Ontario Hockey League rookie of the year voting behind John Tavares and Logan Couture.

His stock climbed higher the following year when he played on a line with Patrick Kane and Sam Gagner. Kostitsyn had 40 goals and 91 assists in 59 games to rank third in Canadian Hockey League scoring behind Kane and Tavares.

I was in London to watch a playoff game against Erie and saw Kostitsyn play an incredible shift. Coach Dale Hunter sent Kostitsyn and Gagner out to kill a penalty. They were on the ice for the full two minutes, and Kostitsyn stayed on the ice to score a goal 1:38 later.

Coaches tend to get upset when players stay on the ice too long, and I suggested to Hunter that the goal might have saved Kostitsyn from a lecture.

Not at all, said the coach.

"If those guys on the top line aren't out there for at least 30 minutes a game, we don't have a chance," said Hunter.

After his brilliant junior career, there was an expectation that Sergei would be a better pro than his brother, but it didn't work out that way. Sergei had nine goals and 18 assists in 52 games as a rookie in 2007–08, and that would be his best season as a Canadien.

He ran afoul of coach Jacques Martin when he missed the bus for a preseason game in Quebec City in 2009. His excuse was that he was caught in traffic. That might have been believable if the bus hadn't been leaving at 7:00 AM on a Sunday morning. He was suspended twice that season for failing to report to the Canadiens' farm club in Hamilton, and he was left home from a playoff game the following spring after he became involved in a locker-room argument with Carey Price.

Sergei Kostitsyn did find some success after he was traded to Nashville in 2010. He had 23 goals and 27 assists in his first season with the Predators, but his love affair with the NHL and country music soured after the lockout in 2012. He had a year remaining on his contract with the Predators, but they released him in 2013 so he could go to the KHL.

Any desire to keep Sergei probably vanished during a March 17, 2013, game in Edmonton. The Predators were on the power play when Kostitsyn lost the puck to former teammate Sam Gagner. Kostitsyn didn't make any attempt at pursuit on the play, and the Oilers scored a shorthanded goal that was the difference in a 3–2 Edmonton win.

The Kostitsyns fell into the category of players who love Montreal too much. They frequented the city's high-end bars and restaurants, and it's safe to say they had more success with women than the Festrunk brothers.

In 2009, their lifestyle caught them in the crosshairs of Project Axe, a Montreal police investigation into a drug trafficking ring with ties to the infamous Hells Angels motorcycle gang.

Police surveillance revealed that the brothers spent a lot of time with Pasquale Mangiola, who was arrested for drug and weapons trafficking and conspiracy in a criminal enterprise. Police reports indicated that Mangiola, a self-described hockey nut, helped the brothers negotiate deals for cars and high-end electronics, introduced them to women, and, on occasion, delivered vodka to their homes.

The brothers denied any wrongdoing and were never charged with any criminal offense.

When Andrei Kostitsyn was asked about the association with Mangiola, he replied: "It's a crazy story. We're from Belarus, you think we need help to find vodka?"

Andrei Kostitsyn played an indirect role in Alex Radulov joining the Canadiens in 2016. Radulov returned from the KHL to play for Nashville in the 2012 playoffs. He had a goal and five assists in eight games, but his comeback ended abruptly when he and Andrei Kostitsyn were busted for missing curfew before Game 2 of the Predators' second-round series against Phoenix.

There was one report that Kostitsyn had been spotted in a Scottsdale bar at 5:00 AM, but it's more likely that the pair was only an hour late and that a check of the electronic door records led to their downfall.

Someone in the Nashville organization was privy to the information, but coach Barry Trotz wasn't informed before the game. Kostitsyn scored a goal that night and Radulov had an assist, but once their transgression became public, they were sent packing and Radulov had to wait another four years before getting another chance at the NHL.

Sticking Up for a Teammate

I was sleeping in a beachside hotel on Sand Key north of St. Petersburg on February 11, 2008, when my phone pinged to indicate that I had a message. I glanced at my watch, saw that it was few minutes before 6:00 AM, and figured that if someone was sending me a message at that time it might be important.

I didn't recognize the number, and the message simply read: Check your email.

I booted up my computer, and there was a link to a Tampa police report. Canadiens defenseman Ryan O'Byrne had been arrested for grand theft while teammate Tom Kostopoulos had been charged with resisting arrest without violence.

I took the scant details in the report, posted the story on the *Montreal Gazette* website, and headed to the Tampa police station. When I arrived at the station, I learned that the two players had been released two hours earlier after several of their teammates—captain Saku Koivu, Chris Higgins, and Cristobal

Huet—had posted bail. O'Byrne was released on $2,000 bail, and Kostopoulos' bail was set at $500.

The next stop was the team hotel, where the media had started to gather. There was no sign of the players, but a team spokesman confirmed that there had been "an incident" and that General Manager Bob Gainey and the players would address the issue after practice that afternoon.

"My message is that this is serious business," said Gainey, who learned of the incident when he arrived in Tampa at 9:00 AM. "It's a shame that it happened. It's not a pleasant event. It happened during an annual team dinner. Unfortunately we can't go back, we must go forward. We will try to diminish and also eliminate the negative effects this story will have on our team."

Both players said they apologized to their teammates but said they had been advised by lawyers not to discuss the incident.

"After our team meeting, Bob Gainey reminded us all there was a lesson to be learned from this incident," said Kostopoulos. "I am happy the team decided not to punish us."

Head coach Guy Carbonneau called the incident "deplorable" and something you never like to hear about, but he said he had to get the Canadiens ready to play the Tampa Bay Lightning the following night.

"We are in 2008, it's not the first year something like this has happened," Carbonneau said. "The two players were not suspended, but I haven't decided yet if they will play against Tampa Bay. We met with them to hear their version. We wanted to know the truth. It's too bad, but at least no one got hurt."

For the record, Kostopoulos did not play in a 3–2 loss to the Lightning. O'Byrne was dressed, but that might have been a case of necessity because defenseman Roman Hamrlik missed the game with the flu.

So what really happened that night?

It took weeks for the details to emerge, but, although they may have been misguided, both players were coming to the defense of a teammate.

The evening began with the team's annual rookie dinner at Bern's Steakhouse, a Tampa institution known for its prime beef and a wine list, which runs to hundreds of pages. O'Byrne, who had been recalled from Hamilton a week earlier, shared the cost of the dinner with fellow rookies Carey Price and Sergei Kostitsyn.

After dinner, the party moved up South Howard Avenue to Whiskey Park, a popular nightclub. The good times began to unravel when a woman used her cell phone to take a picture of a Canadiens player in a compromising situation.

O'Byrne made it his responsibility to secure the phone with the pictures. He started talking to the woman and saw his opportunity when she went to the ladies' room and asked O'Byrne to watch her purse.

Before he had a chance to grab the phone, the club's bouncers came through the bar and announced that the bar was closing and everyone had to leave immediately. O'Byrne grabbed the purse and went outside to wait for the woman.

When the woman returned to the bar, there was no sign of her purse or O'Byrne, and she started to scream that she has been robbed. As it happened, the Tampa police were already on the scene investigating another incident. A former professional basketball player had arrived at the club earlier in the night to find his girlfriend with another man, and he reacted by going into the parking lot and jumping up and down on the hood of his rival's Mercedes-Benz.

The police went outside where they found O'Byrne holding the purse and the cell phone.

"What are you doing with that purse?" they asked.

"It's my girlfriend's, I'm waiting for her," replied O'Byrne.

Unfortunately, he didn't have an answer when they asked him for his girlfriend's name.

When the police directed O'Byrne to the backseat of a cruiser, several Montreal players tried to intervene, explaining that O'Byrne had made an honest mistake. Most of the players backed off when the police offered them an opportunity to join O'Byrne at the police station.

But Kostopoulos, who had a reputation for coming to the aid of his teammates on the ice, continued to plead O'Byrne's case and was arrested.

The arrests could have jeopardized the players' ability to enter the United States, but both charges were eventually dropped. The charges against Kostopoulos were dropped in April after he wrote a letter apologizing to the police. O'Byrne was let off the hook in July after he apologized to the woman and agreed to do community service in Canada.

Staying Out Late

Most coaches today rarely impose a curfew on their players.

"There are certain situations where you might have a curfew, but generally you expect the players to be responsible and show some common sense," noted Canadiens coach Claude Julien.

That wasn't always the case.

Hall of Fame coach Scotty Bowman was a great believer in the adage early to bed, early to rise. While he credits Chicago's Rudy Pilous with introducing the morning skate in 1961, Bowman used morning skates as a measure to ensure that his players woke up in the morning.

There's a famous story about Bowman telling the players there would be a $100 fine for any player breaking curfew and Peter Mahovlich responding by taking two $100 bills from his wallet, handing them to Bowman, and saying: "This should cover me for tonight and tomorrow."

When I asked Mahovlich if the story was true, he smiled and said: "Probably."

Bowman loves to tell the story of the night in Detroit when he went to the hotel lobby at midnight and handed the doorman a stick.

"I told him he could get the players' autographs and it would be a nice souvenir. The next morning I went down and checked the names on the stick. The stick cost $20, but I got a couple of hundred dollars in fines."

I had an interesting late-night encounter with a couple of players the night before a game in Chicago. I went to see a Chicago Bulls game and returned to the Drake Hotel a little before midnight. I decided to go around the corner to Dublin, an Irish pub that offers a perfect pint of Guinness and a kitchen that stays open until 4:00 AM.

As I walked in, I noticed two Canadiens players sitting at the bar with two young ladies. I sensed a bit of panic on their faces as they spotted me, but I merely nodded and walked to the other end of the bar.

Minutes later, one of the players approached me and said: "Hey Pat, we're cool, eh?"

"Don't worry," I assured him. "I'm here to get a beer and a sandwich. I don't care what you guys do."

It was shortly after 2:00 AM when the players and the women got up and prepared to leave but not before I received another visit from the player.

After assuring him that this was our little secret, he asked me: "Hey Pat, how come you're here?"

"Well, I felt like a beer, and I don't have to worry about playing a game tomorrow," I replied.

"No, I mean why did you come to this bar?" he asked.

I pointed to one of the stained-glass windows and said: "You see that thing that looks like a clover? That's a shamrock. That's an Irish symbol, this is an Irish bar, and I'm Irish. If you don't want to run into me, don't go into any bars with shamrocks on the window."

I didn't give the encounter any more thought until the next afternoon as we waited for the bus to take us to the United Center.

A player walked over to me said: "I hear you were out late last night."

"Where did you hear that?"

"A little birdie told me."

"Well, tell the little birdie he's dumber than I thought. It's one thing to break the rules and cheat on your team, but it's not something you should brag about."

But my favorite story about a missed curfew dates back to 1941 and involved Paul Haynes and Coach Dick Irvin. Haynes, who twice finished in the top 10 in scoring, was a rarity because he had a degree from Montreal's Loyola College, where he played hockey and was the star quarterback on the football team.

Irvin cut Haynes from the team after he missed a curfew in New York because he was at the opera.

It was Downhill for Vlad

One of the drawbacks of playing for the Canadiens is that you are instantly recognizable, and if you should happen to step out of line, there's a good chance that someone will blow the whistle on you.

That was the case for defenseman Vladimir Malakhov when he decided to take his family to Mont-Tremblant for a few days of skiing during the 2000 All-Star Game break.

There were a couple of problems with the trip. For starters, Malakhov had a clause in his contract that stipulated that he wasn't supposed to ski during the season.

And then there was the fact that Malakhov hadn't played a single game in the 1999–2000 season because he was recovering from knee surgery. He had returned to practice, and coach Alain Vigneault, who was not a huge Malakhov fan, was waiting for the Russian to tell him he was ready. "He has to knock on my door, then we have to ask the doctor for the green light, and then we'll make a decision," Vigneault said. "He hasn't knocked on my door. Maybe he didn't have time."

When pictures surfaced of Malakhov on the slopes, Vigneault confronted him. Malakhov admitted he had been skiing, but said he was only on the gentler slopes with his son. The Canadiens immediately suspended him and said he would be reinstated when he was cleared to play.

Malakhov insisted he did nothing wrong.

"I didn't do anything dangerous," he said. "I do things more dangerous than that on the ice in practice. I'm not that stupid to risk missing another year. I ski every year. I skied last year, the year before, and the year before that.

"This time I got caught. But I wasn't the only one. Today, I'm the villain, but I've had it up to here with all these stories."

Team captain Saku Koivu supported Vigneault's decision.

"I think they have all the reasons to do it," he said. "Maybe it wasn't the smartest thing to do. I don't think it was right for the guys—in one way I don't think he should have done that. But at the same time, nothing happened."

The suspension lasted only a few days, but Malakhov's days in Montreal were numbered. After failing to pick up a point in seven games, Malakhov was traded to New Jersey for Sheldon Souray, Josh DeWolf, and a draft pick.

General Manager Réjean Houle insisted that the skiing trip didn't trigger the deal. While Malakhov was an extremely talented player and a physical force, he never seemed comfortable playing hockey, and Vigneault questioned his commitment.

Houle said he talked to several teams about a deal before Malakhov went skiing. He noted Malakhov was eligible to become a free agent at the end of the season, and the New Jersey deal allowed the Canadiens to pick up a couple of young defensemen.

For the record, Souray became a force on the Canadiens' power play, while DeWolf never played a single game in the NHL.

He'll Always Have Paris

Veteran defenseman Patrice Brisebois is another player who landed in hot water because he was in the wrong place at the wrong time.

The Brisebois saga began during the pregame warmup for a game at the Air Canada Centre on February 8, 2003. The defenseman experienced chest pains and left the ice. David Mulder, the Canadiens' team physician, detected an irregular heartbeat and was concerned enough that he sent Brisebois to a Toronto hospital for tests.

When the Canadiens flew home that night after losing 3–1, Brisebois remained in the hospital with arrhythmia. After two days of tests and observation, Brisebois was sent home. Dr. Mulder said there was no sign of damage to the heart and that Brisebois' problems were related to stress.

The diagnosis made sense because the Canadiens were struggling on the ice, and Brisebois, the highest-paid player on the Montreal roster, bore the brunt of the criticism from the fans and media.

Earlier in the week, the Canadiens dropped a 4–3 decision to Atlanta at the Bell Centre, and Brisebois contributed to the loss when he made a bad pass while trying to avoid a check. Dan Snyder picked off the pass and set up Jeff Cowan for the goal.

Montreal Gazette columnist Jack Todd described it this way: "Of course, it was no surprise that Brisebois chose to avoid contact. When he coughed up the puck to Dan Snyder Tuesday night and left Jeff Cowan unattended in front, it was one of those spectacular fluffs that will make the highlight reel the day Brisebois retires.

"Brisebois looked like a man about to be run over by a Porsche when he bailed. A sensible play, maybe, but not remotely what Brisebois is paid to do."

When Brisebois was released from the hospital, he was told to rest and stay away from the rink. He took the advice literally, boarding a flight to Paris where there was no debate over whether he was worth the money the Canadiens were paying him.

There was one problem—he didn't tell the Canadiens he was going, and management was blindsided when *La Presse* reported that several fans spotted Brisebois on the flight.

Brisebois spent five days in France and returned to speculation that he would be traded. The rumors were fuelled by news that Brisebois' home was on the market.

While Brisebois' absence was an embarrassment to the team, General Manager André Savard said Brisebois would not be punished. He blamed the incident on a breakdown in communication.

Fellow defenseman Stéphane Quintal tried to interject some humor into the situation.

"I haven't talked to him, but I think he felt he had to get away from all the talk, and you can't do that at home in Montreal or at Mont Tremblant," said Quintal. "It was either Paris or Plattsburgh."

Mariusz Czerkawski said the constant booing Brisebois had been exposed to may have taken its toll on the veteran.

"We're not machines, and it hurts when the fans boo you all the time," said Czerkawski.

Brisebois resumed practicing two days after his return from Paris, but it was clear that he was out of shape after 10 days off the ice. He missed seven games before returning.

CHAPTER 14
ON THE JOB

When I tell people what I do for a living, their first question is usually: "Do you get to go to all the games?"

More often than not, I jokingly reply: "No, I *have* to go to all the games."

Covering sports is a job, although I have to agree with colleague Michael Farber, who is fond of saying we have the best job in the world.

We're paid to watch games and comment on them. But there are the frustrations that come with any job. You go through the same 82-game grind as the players—minus the chartered flights, expedited trips through customs, and someone to look after your laundry. But, just like the players, there are nights when you struggle for a lead. There are nights when you know you should be in bed with a mug of NeoCitran, but instead you're shuttling between a chilly arena and an overheated hotel room.

You aren't supposed to root for the team you cover, but you are aware that your job is easier when the team is winning. Those are the nights when you ask a player about scoring the winning goal instead of trying to find the player who is hiding in the clinic so he doesn't have to explain why he turned the puck over in his own end.

The business has changed over the years. When I started, reporters carried portable typewriters on road trips and found telegraph operators to transmit a story back to the paper. Today, we have laptops and cell phones. When Carey Price signed his four-year extension in 2012, I recorded his conference call on my phone and filed the story using the wifi at a McDonald's in rural Virginia.

In the Original Six era, travel was by train, and reporters accompanied the team. We continued to accompany the team when it started traveling by charter, but GM Bob Gainey kicked us off the plane in 2003.

Colleague Red Fisher contracted pneumonia after we made the move to commercial flights and accused Gainey to trying to kill him. But the culprit in this case was the company's designated travel agent, which sent him from Tampa to Montreal via Houston and Chicago.

The media contingent covering the team has grown over the years.

I can recall sitting in Toe Blake's office with two other reporters after practice. Today, with the proliferation of all-sports TV and radio networks, websites and the team's own TV and web presence, there can be up to 40 people at the coach's press conference.

Player scrums in the dressing room are more chaotic. The Canadiens rarely provide access to more than two or three players at a time, and there is a battle for space as cameramen try to get their shot and reporters shove microphones into the player's face. The jockeying for position can get rough, and, in 2004, a fight broke out between a radio reporter and a TV reporter. The highlight of the day was captain Saku Koivu standing on a bench to get a better view.

Here are some stories about good times and bad times on the road.

Dining High on the Hog

The game-day ritual for the media includes the pregame meal, which is as much a social event as a culinary experience. The meals, which are provided by the teams for a price ranging from

$5 to $15, are a chance to mingle with the opposing media, scouts, and team personnel.

John Bartlett, the play-by-play voice of the Canadiens' telecasts on TSN, is the resident gourmand among the traveling media, and he has set up a rating system for the pregame meals.

"Carolina used to be the runaway winner until they cut back on the cobbler," said Bartlett. "They still have the ice-cream machine, but I miss the cobbler for dessert."

As you would expect, barbecue is big in Carolina, and the main attraction is pulled pork with a choice of vinegar or tomato-based sauces. There's also a roast being sliced as well as a chicken dish, veggies, soup, and sweet tea.

Once upon a time, there was a fruit cobbler and banana cream pie in Carolina, but they disappeared in what was described as a cost-cutting move. That opened up the top spot, and there's an ongoing debate over the relative merits of the variety in Tampa Bay and Calgary's ability to do one thing very well.

The meal in Tampa kicks off with the best salad bar in the league, a choice of soups, a local dish, some chicken, and a pasta station where the chef offers a choice of pastas, sauces, and goodies such as shrimp, chicken, sausage, and fresh vegetables.

There's only one main course in Calgary, but it's a roast of prime Alberta beef, which would do any steakhouse proud. It is not only the tastiest meal in the league, but it's also the least expensive at $5.

Chicago overwhelms the media with two meals. There's the pregame meal, and then there's a second offering in the press box after the second period, which offers roasted vegetables for the virtuous and Chicago-style sausages for everyone else.

The offerings in Detroit include Little Caesars pizza, a natural since the Illich family owns the Red Wings and the pizza chain. Boston and Buffalo are two cities that have stepped up their culinary games in recent years, and, while Montreal is known for its fine restaurants, the media meal at the Bell Centre is somewhere in the middle of the pack. In between a good salad bar and ice cream for dessert, there are uninspired pasta dishes and some take on meat or fish. The chef runs into the most trouble when he goes ethnic and screws up such classics as Indian butter chicken, Greek moussaka, or the Chinese-American staple General Tso's chicken. The Canadiens do get it right on Super Bowl weekend as they go to brunch mode with crepes and cooked-to-order omelets accompanying pig three ways—ham, bacon, and sausage. The Canadiens also offer grilled hot dogs between periods.

Back in olden days, there was also beer—Molson's of course— in the Montreal press room, and there was a bottle of Chivas Regal stashed away in the back for Red Fisher, who enjoyed a shot prior to the game. The beer disappeared sometime in the 1990s over concern that members of the media might drink too much and run afoul of the law, but the bottle of Chivas remained in place until Fisher retired in 2012.

For years, the absolute worst press box meal was the one served up by the New York Islanders, and things have improved only slightly since the move to Barclays Center.

Ottawa isn't known for its meals, but one of the highlights in the team's early years were the fresh baked cookies for dessert. The cookies proved so popular that there were no cookies left when General Manger Pierre Gauthier showed up for dinner before a game in the mid-1990s. Gauthier immediately instituted a one-cookie policy.

No Love in Philly

Philadelphia bills itself as the City of Brotherly Love, but the message is lost on the city's hyperactive sports fans. They have a reputation for being unruly and obnoxious, and, as I discovered during the 2010 Eastern Conference Final, destructive.

After the Canadiens posted a 5–1 win for Game 3 on May 20, I filed my story and went to the parking lot of the Wells Fargo Center to retrieve my Honda Accord, a road warrior with more than 300,000 miles on the odometer. There were few cars left in the lot, and, as I approached the vehicle, I noticed that there were a number of beer cans on the hood and the roof. When I reached the car, I realized the empty cans were the least of my problems.

One of the hubcaps had been broken off, one windshield wiper was missing, and another was bent out of shape. There was a crack running down one side of the windshield.

As I circled the car I noticed, the rear tire on the driver's side was flat, and when I went to check on my spare tire, I noticed that the license plate was missing.

The security guards at the arena called AAA, and a call to the Philadelphia police provided me with an address where I could file a police report in the morning.

The next day was busy. Between practices, I filed a police report, bought a new tire and wipers and called Canada Customs for assurance that I could get back into the country without a license plate.

By the time I arrived for the morning skate the next day, the story of the vandalism had gone viral. A Philadelphia TV station interviewed me, and there were stories in the local papers. The wire services picked up the saga, and I received hundreds of emails. Some said I was the cause of my misfortune because I was dumb enough to drive to Philadelphia. The overwhelming majority of the emails were from Philadelphia residents who sympathized with my plight and said they hoped I wouldn't judge the entire city based on this one incident. There were offers of meals, drinks, and tours of the city.

My return home after Game 4 was interesting. I was stopped by the police in Pennsylvania, New Jersey, and twice in New York because I was driving without a plate. I expected another delay when I reached the border crossing in Lacolle, Quebec. As I pulled up to the inspection booth, the officer said: "Do you know you don't have a licence plate?"

As I started to explain, he looked at my passport and said: "Mr. Hickey, I'm sorry; we heard all about your problems. Welcome back."

I didn't expect the Philadelphia police to follow up with an investigation. I figured the police report was merely a formality for my insurance company, but a couple of factors led to an arrest.

For starters, the police took these incidents seriously. While Philadelphians bristle whenever people talk about Santa Claus being pelted with snowballs during a Christmas parade—apparently Kris Kringle had been into the egg nog—the city has a history of unruly fans. The situation became so bad at Philadelphia Eagles games that the city has set up a temporary courthouse at the stadium to deal with miscreants.

My experience with vandalism came close on the heels of two other incidents.

One was fairly benign. A college student who had too much to drink and an appetite for his 15 minutes of notoriety, jumped on the field during a Phillies game and led police on a merry chase. Before embarking on his adventure, he called his father and told him to watch the game, but TV networks have a policy of turning a blind camera to such shenanigans.

A far more serious incident involved a drunken 21-year-old fan. He and a friend were ejected from a Phillies game after two Mets fans—an off-duty police officer and his 11-year-old daughter—complained about their unruly behaviour. As the fan was leaving, he paused, stuck two fingers down his throat and vomited on the girl.

Social media kicked the investigation of my case into high gear. One of the people involved posted a picture of my license plate on Instagram, and one of his friends put it on his Facebook page with the message: "I wonder how this guy's getting home."

The police homed in on the Facebook poster, and, at one point, he sent me a message saying that I had ruined his life.

Eventually, the original post on Instagram led to an arrest, and I received a bizarre call from someone in the Philadelphia district attorney's office.

"Are you a French Canadian?" he asked.

"No," I replied.

The prosecutor was disappointed with my reply, and he went on to explain that I had put the kibosh on the plans to charge the vandal with a hate crime, which seemed to be the definition of prosecutorial overreach.

The vandal was convicted of mischief. I suspect he took the fall for a group of fans who had too much to drink and thought they were having some fun. He was spared jail time but was ordered to make restitution. For the next 13 months I received checks from the court in Philadelphia, which I passed on to a few of my favorite charities.

I've put as many as 35,000 miles a year on my cars. Part of that mileage is the 120-mile commute between my country estate in the Eastern Townships of Quebec and Montreal, but I also take a lot of road trips by car.

There's a perception that I hate flying, but nothing can be further from the truth. I love to fly—I hate dealing with airports and airlines.

And I love to drive. I find it relaxing to get behind the wheel with my radio tuned to NPR and a stack of CDs handy for those times when the reception is iffy. I have the freedom to stop and view Niagara Falls on the way to Buffalo or to check out the new restaurant everyone is talking about in the Hudson Valley. A trip to Boston offers an opportunity to save on wine at one of the large New Hampshire Liquor Commission stores conveniently located along the interstate.

An eight-hour drive to Detroit may seem excessive, but I can break it up with a stop in Toronto to visit my older daughter and my two granddaughters.

I can make my own schedule and not have to worry about a flight cancellation or being bumped because the flight is overbooked.

I've driven as far as Carolina and Columbus, but, as I've grown older, the trips have become shorter. I'll drive to Philadelphia but not to Washington. The six-hour drive to Buffalo is a no-brainer if only because there are no direct flights from Montreal to Buffalo, and flying can mean six hours in airports and in the air.

That's not to say that I haven't run into some problems. There have been flat tires, a blown engine, and the occasional weather-related delay.

On one occasion, I planned to fly to games in Columbus and Detroit. I had a Tuesday afternoon flight to Columbus, but I was informed on Monday that the flight had been canceled because a storm was moving up the Atlantic Coast and they were expecting problems in Philadelphia where I was scheduled to make the connection to Columbus.

United had rebooked me on a late afternoon flight on Wednesday, but the game was a 7:00 PM start and there was no margin for error if the flight was late.

After checking the weather, I hopped into my car on Tuesday morning and made a long but uneventful trip to Columbus, traveling north and west of the storm's path.

I had no problem Thursday when I made the relatively short trip from Columbus to Detroit.

But there were problems Saturday morning when I attempted to return to Montreal for a game that night. A storm had created some problems on the 500-mile stretch of Highway 401 from Detroit to the Quebec border. I was reassured that Canadians know how to deal with snow, and the first half of the trip went smoothly. I was three hours from home when the problems began.

Traffic slowed to a crawl. There was an accident ahead, but a report on the radio said emergency crews were on the scene and only a minimal delay was expected.

A half-hour later, I found myself parked on the highway. The accident had closed a stretch of the highway—I later learned that the situation worsened when two fire trucks and an ambulance had joined the 37-vehicle pileup—and I had to wait more than an hour to exit to a series of country roads that weren't equipped to handle a parade of lumbering trucks and three lanes of traffic, which had been reduced to one. My three-hour cushion for the 7:00 PM start had disappeared by the time I pulled back onto the highway.

I was still 90 minutes away when I did my pregame radio show on TSN–690, and I listened to the first period on the radio. I called my colleague Brenda Branswell and told her that I was running late, and she assured me that everything was under control. She was a relative newcomer to the beat and had never written a game story. But she was a veteran reporter, and I assured her that she was up to the task. When I finally reached Montreal, the game was in the second period. I called Brenda and told her I was heading home.

The Flight from Hell

Hockey is a winter sport, and, while you can expect some weather-related delays, nothing prepared me for the events of January 12, 2017.

The Canadiens played in Winnipeg on January 11 and were playing in Minnesota the next night. The flight from Winnipeg to Minnesota takes slightly more than hour, and I booked a 7:30 AM flight, which would allow me to attend the Wild's morning skate and have a pregame nap.

It was below zero Fahrenheit and it was snowing lightly when I left my hotel shortly after 5:00 AM. Twenty minutes later, it was snowing a little harder as I arrived at the airport, and there was a full-scale blizzard when we boarded the plane.

We started to taxi to the deicing pad when the pilot informed us that the airport had been closed because of the storm. There was a further complication because the airport's wind gauges weren't functioning properly.

The pilot headed the plane back to the gate, only to be informed that an incoming flight had moved into our original gate. We sat on the plane for an hour before returning to the terminal.

"Looking at the weather report, we should be leaving around two o'clock," said the woman at the Delta counter. "While you're waiting, we'll bring some Tim Horton's coffee and donuts."

The donuts—four dozen to be shared among 70 passengers—arrived a few minutes later, but I wasn't inclined to join the horde. I called Budget in Minnesota and told them to hold my rental car and settled in a quiet corner to read a book.

At 11:30, the woman from Delta said sandwiches were on the way. That was followed 10 minutes later by an announcement that the snow was easing, the wind gauge was fixed, and we would be leaving at noon.

As we lined up to board, about two dozen sandwiches arrived, but again I didn't feel any need to eat because I expected to land in time for a late lunch.

Shortly after noon, everyone was buckled in, and the pilot was ready to go.

Not really.

There was a lurch as the plane attempted to back out of the gate. It was followed by another jolt. And another.

"Ladies and gentleman, we have a problem," said the captain. "Our brakes are frozen, but it's not a major problem. We'll get a little heat on them we'll be out of here in no time."

Shortly after 2:00, we were able to move. I called Budget a second time to make sure they held my car and looked forward to an early dinner.

As we made our second journey to the deicing pad, the captain was back. It seems that the aeronautical equivalent of the check engine light had come on and we were once again headed back to the terminal.

"The good news is we don't think it's serious," said the captain. "The bad news is that we need two mechanics to sign off on the problem. One is here; the second is 30 minutes away. Just sit tight and we'll get going."

At 3:30 PM, the captain was back. This time, the news was not good. They were asking everyone to gather their belongings. He suggested that we look into booking flights for tomorrow.

I called Budget and told them to cancel the car I asked them to hold.

As we prepared to exit the plane, there was yet another announcement. The problem had been fixed, and we would be taking off—after the paperwork had been okayed at Delta's head office in Atlanta.

We finally lifted off a few minutes before five o'clock, and I was glad that I hadn't checked my bag and that I would be able to grab a taxi as soon as I arrived in Minnesota.

We landed at 6:10, and 10 minutes later, I was in a taxi heading to St. Paul. Between the snow and rush hour, it was touch-and-go for a 7:00 PM start, but I arrived in the press box in time to hear the anthems.

As I settled in my seat, I noticed that Jean-François Chaumont, my confrere from *Le Journal de Montréal*, hadn't arrived. I was sure he had left the plane ahead of me, and I began to worry when he hadn't arrived by the end of the first period.

He arrived in time for the second period, and he added another episode to the saga. His cab was seven blocks from the arena when its transmission broke. Chaumont felt he shouldn't have to pay for the ride, and there was a stalemate when the driver refused to get Chaumont's luggage out of the truck until he paid.

By this time, I was starving, and I was happy to hear there would be snacks in the press box between periods. I was less happy when the snacks turned out to be tater tots with Cheez Wiz.

I passed on the tater tots, and, shortly after midnight, with my story filed, tweets tweeted, and emails answered, I bellied up to the bar at Tom Reid's Hockey City Pub and ate a pecan crusted walleye washed down by a Surly Furious IPA.

It was the perfect ending to a not-so-perfect day.

Don't Mention Overtime

I'm often asked when I file my story, and the answer is within minutes of the final siren.

My deadline for a first-edition game story is 10:30. If the game has a 7:00 PM start, I have a few extra minutes to file the story, although I still have to be aware that, in a perfect world, the locker room will be open for interviews five minutes after the last player leaves the ice, and I have to be there.

Since this isn't a perfect world, I usually have a few extra minutes.

There's more pressure with a 7:30 start, and, if the game starts at 8:00 PM, I usually have to rely on the editors back at the office to find a few extra minutes for me.

Reporters love blowouts. If one team goes ahead by three or four goals, it provides an opportunity to write the story and have it ready to go as soon as soon as the game ends.

Overtime games are a nightmare, particularly when the tying goal is scored in the final minutes of regulation. By that time, you've written a lead with one team winning, and that's followed by a paragraph or two on the significance of the result. With an overtime game, there's a 50-50 chance those paragraphs will be useless.

When a game goes into overtime, I reach into my computer and pull up my standard OT lead:

"XXXXXX scored at X:XX of overtime to give the XXXXX XXXXX a X–X win over the XXXXXXX Saturday night at the Bell Centre."

If the teams get through five minutes without a goal, I pull up my standard shootout lead:

"XXXXXXX scored the winning goal in a shootout to give the XXXXX XXXXX a X–X win over the XXXXXXX Saturday night at the Bell Centre."

I can recall one night in Atlanta where the Canadiens ran up a 5–1 lead on the Thrashers, and I confidently started writing about the Montreal victory.

When the Thrashers scored a goal early in the third period, I recorded it with a single line. When the Thrashers scored another goal, I wrote that the home team made the final score look respectable.

Suddenly, it was 5–4, and I gave the home team credit for not giving up and providing the Canadiens with a scare.

The basic premise of the story, a strong Canadiens' victory on the road, disappeared when Atlanta scored the tying goal with minutes to play.

When Ilya Kovalchuk scored the winner in overtime, I had to scramble to make sense of a story predicated on an easy Montreal win.

I shared the elevator down to the event level with Thrashers general manager Don Waddell, who asked:

"Did you have enough to write about tonight?"

"Too much," I replied.

The Ice Storm of 1998

When the Canadiens arrived at the Bell Centre to play the Boston Bruins on January 7, 1998, they were greeted by thousands of empty seats.

Montreal was in the third day of a crippling ice storm, which knocked out power for millions of Quebecers and caused damage in the $5–6 billion range. Roads had turned to sheer ice, Montreal's Metro was experiencing frequent power outages, and many fans decided to stay home.

The weather posed an immediate problem for the Canadiens. They were scheduled to play the following night on Long Island and were scheduled to fly to New York immediately after their 2–1 overtime loss. They boarded the team bus and arrived at Trudeau Airport to find that all flights had been grounded. Team officials were told it was likely they would be able to fly the next morning, and they scrambled to find hotel rooms near the airport.

A streetscene in Montreal in January 1998, just after the historic ice storm. Here, a woman makes her way past huge blocks of ice while crossing the street as trucks attempt clean-up operations. *(AP Photo/Paul Chiasson)*

I was driving to New York, and I planned to get a head start after the game by driving three hours to Saratoga Springs. The weather conditions for the first part of the drive were horrendous, but when I reached the mountains south of Plattsburgh, it was snowing, and it turned to light rain as I neared Saratoga.

The next morning, I learned that the Canadiens charter had been delayed, and, by the time I reached New York shortly after noon, the plane was still on the ground in Montreal. When I checked into the Long Island Marriott at 3:00 PM, I was told the flight was taking off, and the Islanders were thinking about moving the start time from 7:00 PM to 7:30.

It was almost 5:30 when the Canadiens arrived at the hotel and began to walk across the parking lot to the Nassau Coliseum.

Coach Alain Vigneault had two concerns as he looked at his weary players. He wasn't sure how they would perform after spending most of the day in the airport, and he wasn't sure the plane would be able to return to Montreal after the game.

He needn't have worried on either account. The Canadiens crushed the Islanders 8–2, and the plane was cleared for the return trip.

I had my own concerns about going home. I lived an hour outside Montreal in an area that avoided most of the damage, but I was concerned about the roads. I planned to skirt the damage by driving east of the storm through New England. I called AAA in Vermont to ask about the state of Interstate 91.

"Where do you want to go?" asked the lady from AAA.

"I'm going to Canada," I replied.

"I'm sorry, you can't go there. It's closed."

The return home was uneventful with the exception of a few detours once I reached Canada, and I began to wonder whether the New York Rangers would be able to fly in for their Saturday night game at the Bell Centre. The Rangers did make it in Friday night, but on Saturday morning, the Canadiens announced that the game would be postponed. The opponents were in town, and the power outage didn't affect the Bell Centre, which had its own generator, but the Canadiens were concerned that their fans would be at risk because of icy sidewalks and ice falling off rooftops.

Shortly after 2:00 PM, the Canadiens called and said they were flying to Florida where they were playing the Lightning the following Tuesday. I was instructed to be at the Bell Centre by 5:30 PM so I could get on the charter, which was leaving from Mirabel Airport north of the city.

Getting to the Bell Centre proved to be a problem. Montreal is an island, and the storm had closed all the main bridges. As I approached the city, there was a radio report that the Champlain Bridge would be opening within the hour. As I lined up for the bridge, I saw a Quebec Provincial Police officer and asked when the bridge would open.

He shrugged and replied: "15 minutes, half an hour, tomorrow."

I took the hint and made a quick detour for the Lafontaine Tunnel near the east end of the island. The traffic was heavy, but I made it onto the island where I encountered another problem—there were no traffic lights. It took me an hour to navigate the 10 miles to the Bell Centre, stopping at each intersection along the way.

I parked my car in the garage beneath the Bell Centre and boarded a bus bound for the largely abandoned airport north of Montreal.

By midnight, we were in our hotel in Tampa. I sat at the bar drinking a margarita and watching a TV news report about the ice storm.

Wait Until Tomorrow

Getting information from coaches or general managers can often be difficult. They are reluctant to discuss injuries, trade rumors, contract negotiations, or lineup changes.

At one coach's press conference, I tried to pin down Michel Therrien on his starting goaltender for the next day's game.

"I'll let you know tomorrow," said Therrien.

"At my age, there's no guarantee I'll be around tomorrow," I replied.

Therrien laughed and then said: "Well, I could tell you now, but, at your age, you'd probably forget."

CHAPTER 15
LIFE AFTER HOCKEY

Getting Political

Serge Savard's nickname was the Senator, and it reflected his statesmanlike bearing, but he declined the many offers to throw his hat into the political ring. Savard was a strong supporter of the Quebec Liberal Party, and the party, in turn, helped him launch his business career by awarding him a franchise to sell provincial lottery tickets.

Another Canadiens captain, Jean Béliveau, also resisted efforts to recruit him for public office. He turned down two offers of an appointment to the Canadian Senate and also declined when Prime Minister Jean Chrétien offered him the post of governor general, the Queen's representative in Canada.

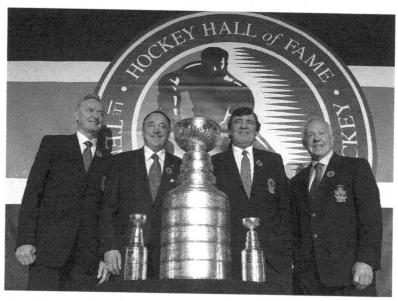

Canadiens legends (from left) Larry Robinson, Frank Mahovlich, Serge Savard, and Yvan Cournoyer pose with the Stanley Cup trophy during the opening of the Montreal Canadiens Centennial Exhibit at the Hockey Hall of Fame in 2008. *(AP Phot/The Canadian Press, Frank Gunn)*

But former goaltender Ken Dryden served as a Member of Parliament for seven years and ran for the leadership of the federal Liberal Party.

And Frank Mahovlich and former Canadiens coach Jacques Demers were both named to the Canadian Senate, an appointed body that reviews bills passed by the House of Commons.

Mahovlich's 14 years in the Senate were uneventful. He was appointed by Liberal Prime Minister Jean Chrétien, and one colleague said you could count the number of speeches Mahovlich made in the Senate on one hand and have fingers left over.

When he reached the mandatory retirement age of 75, Mahovlich's final speech was brief. He thanked Chrétien for appointing him in 1998; his assistants and research staff; his wife, Marie; and finally, "everyone in the Senate and, indeed, in Parliament. I would like to bid adieu to the Senate and leave with these final words: I have had a wonderful time. Thank you."

Demers was appointed by Conservative Prime Minister Stephen Harper in 2009, and it was a bit of a surprise because, four years earlier, in 2005, Demers revealed that he was illiterate.

Demers was aware that he could become the butt of jokes when he went public with his literacy problems, but he said it was important to help other people who were ashamed that they couldn't read. He talked about the anxiety that resulted from growing up with an abusive, alcoholic father and how it affected his performance in school before he dropped out in grade eight. He detailed how he hid the problem for years, relying on friends and his associates to navigate such simple tasks as filling out a lineup card or applying for a driver's license.

"I'd ask for help by saying I left my glasses somewhere or I'd say I was a French guy who didn't quite understand something in English," said Demers. "When I was the general manager in Tampa, I had Jay Feaster draw up the contracts. I had to lie a lot to get by."

In the Senate, Demers has been a strong voice for literacy and programs that highlight the problem of child abuse.

Demers showed his strength of character in 2015 when a scandal erupted over false expense claims in the Senate. Dozens of Senators were questioned about their expenses, and the members accused of taking advantage of lax reporting rules included Mike Duffy and Pamela Wallin, both of whom were high-profile TV news personalities before being named to the Senate.

Demers expressed his dismay at the breach of public trust, and he later announced that he was leaving the Conservative caucus and would sit as an independent.

In April 2016, Demers suffered a stroke, which left him paralyzed on the right side. On September 29, he made his first public appearance since the stroke when he was inducted into the Quebec Sports Hall of Fame.

No Trivial Coach

Jim Montgomery's career as a Canadien was short—five games in the strike-shortened 1994–95 season—but he is still recalled as the answer to the trivia question: Who did the Canadiens get from St. Louis in return for captain Guy Carbonneau?

The trade on August 19, 1994, ended a summer of speculation about Carbonneau's future with the Canadiens. While General Manager Serge Savard insisted that it was part of a strategy to get younger, the trade rumors began swirling after Montreal was eliminated by Boston in the first round of the playoffs.

Patrick Roy was struck by appendicitis during the series. An aggressive course of antibiotics allowed him to avoid surgery, but he did miss one game, and Carbonneau became embroiled in a debate over Roy's role in the team's success.

While coach Jacques Demers said it would be difficult to win without a healthy Roy, Carbonneau pointed out that the Canadiens still had to play the series.

"We have to do our best, no matter who's in goal," said Carbonneau. "Patrick Roy isn't the Canadiens."

The problem was that Roy thought he was the Canadiens, and he wasn't happy with Carbonneau's remarks.

Carbonneau made another mistake a few weeks after the Canadiens were eliminated. He was playing golf with Roy and Vincent Damphousse when they were ambushed by a reporter and a photographer from *Le Journal de Montreal*, a daily tabloid.

Carbonneau felt this represented an invasion of privacy and let his feelings be known by offering the intruders a one-fingered salute. The gesture was recorded for posterity by the photographer and appeared on the paper's front page the following day.

The Canadiens were embarrassed by the incident, and Carbonneau was summoned to the Forum for a meeting with team brass. The result was a public apology to the team's fan base. Savard said Carbonneau made a mistake but that it wouldn't affect his standing with the team.

Thus, it was a surprise when the Canadiens traded Carbonneau. But the bigger surprise was the return. While Montgomery was a

Montreal native whose father, Jim Sr., boxed for Canada in the 1956 Olympics, he was an unknown in his hometown.

He played minor and high school hockey in the city's east end and then played Tier Two junior hockey in Pembroke, Ontario, before heading to the University of Maine.

Montgomery had a legendary career with the Black Bears. In four years, he racked up 301 points in 170 games—the fourth-best total in NCAA history and the best ever in Hockey East. He was the most valuable player in the Frozen Four, scoring three goals as Maine defeated Lake Superior State 5–4 in the final. His linemate that season was Paul Kariya who racked up 100 points in his only season of college hockey. The Maine roster also included brothers Chris and Peter Ferraro and Patrice Tardif, all of whom would play in the NHL. Also headed to the NHL was the goaltending duo of Mike Dunham and Garth Snow. With that lineup, it's no surprise Maine finished the season with a 42–1–2 record.

Montgomery signed with St. Louis as a free agent and scored six goals and added 14 assists as a rookie in the 1993–94 season.

That would be Montgomery's most successful year in the NHL. He was excited by the prospect of joining the Canadiens, but his debut was delayed by the lockout in 1994, and his career in Montreal was brief. He played only five games—he was a healthy scratch for seven others—before he was on his way to Philadelphia.

He was supposed to be part of a blockbuster trade that sent John LeClair, Eric Desjardins, and Gilbert Dionne to the Flyers for Mark Recchi, Mark Lamb, and a third-round draft pick.

But the deal came together quicker than Savard expected. He had put Montgomery on waivers so that he could be sent to the

AHL to get more playing time, and the Flyers claimed him. At the same time, Philadelphia took Lamb off the table.

The trade, which is regarded as one of the worst in the team's history, eventually went through as planned but not before the Canadiens put up cash to obtain Lamb.

Montgomery's stay in Philadelphia was as forgettable as the one in Montreal. He played 13 games over two seasons but did have a couple of very good years in the AHL.

He did leave one mark on the City of Brotherly Love. It was Montgomery who provided the line of Eric Lindros, Mikael Renberg, and LeClair with the nickname the Legion of Doom.

He returned to the NHL for 28 games with San Jose and nine with Dallas and had a stint with Ufa Salavat Yulaev in the Russian League.

He turned to coaching when he returned to North America and established a solid reputation for his work with young players. He started with one season as an assistant coach at Notre Dame, followed by three years in a similar role at RPI.

He made his head coaching debut in 2010 with the Dubuque Fighting Saints, an expansion franchise in the USHL. Montgomery surprised everyone by winning a league title in his first season, and he followed it up with a second title two years later. Among the future NHL players he helped develop were Johnny Gaudreau, Mike Matheson, Zemgus Girgensons, and Will Butcher, who would follow Montgomery to the University of Denver.

Denver came calling in 2013, and Montgomery was an instant success. He took his team to the NCAA tournament in each of his first four seasons and won the NCAA championship in 2017.

Montgomery's success didn't go unnoticed by NHL teams, but Coach Monty made it clear that he could afford to be picky when sorting through job offers.

"I'm happy at Denver and so is my family," said Montgomery. "Would I like to coach in the NHL some day? Maybe, but it would have to be the right deal, the right team, the right organization, the right owner, and the right general manager."

The Florida Panthers, who had gone a tumultuous season, interviewed Montgomery twice following the 2016–17 season, and it was the coach who withdrew his name from consideration.

"We have a good team here at Denver, and I want to continue what I've started here," said Montgomery. He said it was flattering to see the interest from the Panthers, but he wanted to stay put.

All the right ingredients were there for Montgomery a year later. The New York Rangers came calling and so did the Dallas Stars. Quality of life for his family, along with rapport with Dallas GM Jim Nill proved to be the deciding factors, as Coach Monty signed a three-year contract to coach the Stars.

Back to School

Mike Komisarek has always believed in keeping promises, and that's why he returned to the University of Michigan campus in 2015.

After helping the Wolverines reach the NCAA Frozen Four in each of his first two seasons, Komisarek left school to sign with the Canadiens, who had drafted him in the first round in 2001.

When injuries and the physical demands of the game caught up with him, Komisarek decided it was time to keep a promise he had made to his parents years earlier.

"I promised a couple of people, including my parents, that I would eventually go back to school," Komisarek told the Detroit Free Press in a 2015 interview. "They always stressed the importance of school. As thrilled as they were when I signed my first NHL contract, they probably were as equally disappointed that I didn't finish school. This was an opportunity to fulfill that promise, but to also make things right with Coach Berenson and the Michigan hockey program."

Red Berenson, whose 16-year NHL career included four seasons with the Canadiens, was disappointed when Komisarek left Michigan because he felt the 6-foot-3, 235-pounder wasn't ready for the NHL.

"I've had a lot of players leave early over the years, and I have no problem if they're ready," Berenson told me in a 2014 interview. "If a player isn't ready to jump into the NHL right away, then they're better off staying in school. Michael Cammalleri left school the same summer as Komisarek, and they both started in the AHL. Komo had a man's body, but he was still a kid. The Canadiens pulled [Max] Pacioretty out after one year, and he spent two years in the AHL."

"One of the toughest things I had to do was make that phone call and tell him I was leaving school early," Komisarek said. "He was really disappointed, and let me know if I was his son he wouldn't let me go.

"Red always cared about his players on and off the ice. He wants you to play in the NHL. He wants you to be a solid character person as well. This is an opportunity to give back to not only Red but the hockey program and the university, which has given me so much."

In addition to getting back into the classroom, Komisarek rejoined the hockey program as an undergraduate assistant coach.

Coming out of Michigan, Komisarek spent the first two seasons bouncing between the Canadiens and the AHL and played sparingly with the Hamilton Bulldogs in the lockout season of 2004–05.

When the lockout ended, he was paired with Andrei Markov, and, for four seasons, he played his best hockey. He was among the NHL leaders in blocked shot and hits. He owed much of his success to Markov. If Komisarek took himself out of a play with a hit, Markov was there to back him up. If Komisarek had trouble clearing the zone, he had only to find Markov, and the Russian would do the rest.

He earned a reputation as a hard worker, a trait which he learned from his parents, who immigrated to New York from Poland. His father, Roman, built a successful auto repair business on Long Island while his mother, Kathy, played the role of hockey mom. She would drive Mike to early-morning practices and then to school.

In the early stages of the 2005–06 season, General Manager Bob Gainey gave him time off so he could be with his mother, who was dying of cancer. After her death in November, he began wearing a small sticker with the initials KK on the back of his helmet. After the playing of the anthems, he would dedicate each game to his mother by tracing the sign of the cross on the ice with his stick.

When Komisarek became a free agent in 2009, the Canadiens faced a decision. They wanted to keep Komisarek, but they also had to contend with the salary cap. They set his value at $3 million a season.

The Toronto Maple Leafs came along with a better offer. Brian Burke had joined the Leafs midway through the previous season, and he was hoping to repeat his success in Anaheim where he built a Stanley Cup winner that emphasized size and toughness. Komisraek fit that profile, and Toronto signed him to a five-year deal worth $22.5 million. That was $4.5 million a year—50 percent more than the Canadiens' offer.

It turned out to be a bad deal. Komisarek suffered a shoulder injury in his first season in Toronto. He required surgery, which limited him to 34 games and also cost him a chance to represent the United States at the 2010 Olympics.

By his third season, he's spending almost as much time in the press box as he was on the ice. When the lockout ended in 2013, the Leafs gave up on him. He played four NHL games before he was placed on waivers and sent to the AHL. At the end of the season, the Leafs bought out the final year of his contract.

I talked with Komisarek during that final season in Toronto and asked him if he had any regrets about leaving Montreal.

"No," he said. He went on to say that he did what he thought was best for him and his family, and there were about 20 million good reasons for signing with the Leafs.

Ron Powers, the former Michigan assistant coach, proved prophetic when he talked about Komisarek's return to Ann Arbor.

"He was a terrific defenseman in his two years here," Powers said. "He was a guy who earned his stripes by his play without the puck and his physicality and his will.

"He's a passionate player, and that will probably show up being a passionate coach."

In 2017, with his degree in hand, Komisarek joined the Buffalo Sabres as a player development coach.

Mike Komisarek wasn't the only former Canadiens defenseman to head back to school after his playing days ended.

On December 17, 2016, Ryan O'Byrne collected his undergraduate degree from Cornell University's internationally recognized School of Hotel Administration.

It was the culmination of a process that began 13 years earlier when the 19-year-old from Victoria arrived at Cornell in Ithaca, New York, to pursue an Ivy League education and play hockey.

"I always knew I wanted to complete my degree," said O'Byrne, who spent three seasons at Cornell before leaving to sign with the Canadiens. "I started taking online courses through Cornell in 2010, and when I came here in September, I had one semester to complete."

O'Byrne, 32, who played 308 NHL games in Montreal, Colorado, and Toronto, said he faced an adjustment when he returned to the campus.

"Most of the courses involve working in teams, and the people I worked with when I was here before are long gone," said O'Byrne. "I was working with 21-year-olds who must have been wondering who this old guy was.

"It took me two or three weeks to fit in," added O'Byrne. "And it was different being able to concentrate on my classes. When I was here before, I was also thinking about the NHL."

It was interesting that O'Byrne chose to study hotel administration because he was working a summer job as a bellhop at a hotel in Victoria when he learned that the Canadiens drafted him in the third round in 2003.

O'Byrne attended St. Michaels University School, the same private high school that produced basketball star Steve Nash. He played two seasons in the British Columbia Hockey League, and the Canadiens were intrigued by the skinny, 6-foot-5 defenseman. They felt he would bulk up with a few years of college, and he went from 195 pounds to 230.

O'Byrne said he didn't expect to make an immediate jump from college to the NHL. He broke in with the AHL's Hamilton Bulldogs, and his rookie season produced one of his favorite hockey memories.

"We won the Calder Cup with Carey [Price] in goal," said O'Byrne. "We had a great group with [Matt] D'Agostini and [Kyle] Chipchura. It was a great way to break in. I played about 90 games in my three years of college, and then I played 110 my first pro season.

"I had a lot of good memories," O'Byrne recalled. "I remember my first NHL game was against Boston, and I had two assists. Then there were the three nights when they retired the numbers [of Ken Dryden, Larry Robinson, and Bob Gainey]. It was great to be there to watch those ceremonies."

And then there was December 4, 2009, when the Canadiens retired the No. 3 worn by Emile [Butch] Bouchard. At the time, O'Byrne was wearing No. 3, but he literally took the shirt off his back and handed it to Bouchard. O'Byrne reappeared on the ice for the game against the Bruins wearing No. 20.

"It was exciting when we went to the Eastern Conference Final in 2010," O'Byrne said of the run that produced 13 of his 25 NHL playoff appearances.

He was traded to Colorado early the next season, and, while the Avalanche struggled, O'Byrne said it was personally satisfying because he played some of his best hockey.

In 2013, O'Byrne moved to Europe, playing for Lev Prague in the Kontinental Hockey League.

"That was a great experience," said O'Byrne. "The KHL is the second-best league in the world, and we went all the way to the final before losing in Game 7 to Metallurg Magnitogorsk, which was coached by Mike Keenan. Prague was a great city, and I enjoyed playing there."

There was one problem—the Prague team went bankrupt after that season. O'Byrne moved on to Ambri-Piotta in the Swiss League where he was reunited with former Canadiens teammate Francis Bouillon, and spent the next season with HV71 Jonkoping in Sweden.

"I had a lot of injuries those two seasons," said O'Byrne. "I had a hip surgery when I was playing in Switzerland and missed most of the season. And then my last year, I had some other injuries. I only played 28 games, and I knew it was time to retire."

His ailments included a broken nose, a separated shoulder, and a back injury, which prompted a doctor to suggest he find another line of employment.

O'Byrne said he may get involved in the hotel business, but he spent the summer of 2016 taking a securities course in Toronto, and he's planning to add an MBA before making a decision on his future.

CHAPTER 16
FOOTNOTES

Putting in Overtime

It's 8:00 AM on a wintry morning in Winnipeg, and the temperature is hovering below 0 degrees Fahrenheit when equipment manager Pierre Gervais and his staff leave the warmth of the team hotel and begin the 10-minute walk to the MTS Centre.

Hockey people like to talk about the importance of work, and nobody works harder—or longer hours—than the equipment staff.

"We're usually at the rink a little after nine to get things ready for the morning skate," said Gervais, who has been with the Canadiens for more than 30 years. "We make sure all the equipment is in the stalls waiting for the players. I make sure all the skates are sharpened. After the skate, we load up the practice gear for the laundry, and when we're on the road we go to the hotel around one for a pregame meal."

There's time for a nap before returning to the rink around 4:00 PM The pregame chores are similar to the work before the morning skate, and the action intensifies after the game.

"There's always a rush when we're on the road and we have to catch a charter," said Gervais. "We have to get everything done ASAP, and that Winnipeg trip was a little more difficult because we were playing the next night in Minnesota. We had to get all the equipment on a truck, drive to airport to meet the plane, go through customs, and make sure everything is loaded."

Everything is a lot of stuff.

"When I started in 1987, we'd go to Quebec City, and we could load everything into an Econoline van," said Gervais. "Now, we would need two of those. Players don't have more equipment, but it takes more to play the game. We have medical stuff, training equipment like weights and mats, coaches' stuff, and video equipment. We carry some TV stuff for RDS.

"There's so many different kinds of underwear these days that we have a separate bag filled with backup underwear," said Gervais. "We bring our own skate sharpener, glove dryers, even a machine to stitch equipment. We have 70-something pieces we carry. When you're on the road, you might not have the same space and you might have things stored in two or three smaller rooms and you check two or three times to make sure you haven't left anything behind."

While the players get off the plane in Minnesota and head for the team hotel, Gervais and his staff have work to do. They load a truck supplied by the home team and ride to the arena where they unload the equipment in preparation for the next day.

"We don't have to worry about the laundry, the home team takes care of that, but we have to make sure everything else is ready," said Gervais. "We unpack the gear, put the players' equipment in their stalls, arrange the sticks. It takes about 45 minutes, but it's late at night and we're back at the hotel at 2:30 or 3:00."

In case you weren't paying attention, that's a 17-, 18-hour day.

"We get a break the next morning because usually only a few guys skate when we have back-to-back games," said Gervais. "We get to the rink around 9:30 and I do the skates and Pat [Langlois] and Steamer [Pierre Ouellette] get the other stuff. If any repairs are needed, that's usually Pat's job. If anything has to be stitched, we have a machine for that at the Bell Centre and another one in Brossad and we have a smaller one we take on the road. The rest of the day is pretty much the same. A good meal, a nap—a good solid hour—and back to the rink. And then we're back on the plane after the game, going home or to the next city. Those back-to-back games can be tough. It's tough on everyone."

With the exception of two train trips to Ottawa, the Canadiens do all their travel on chartered aircraft, and Gervais said that makes his job easier.

"When we used to fly commercial, we'd go to Los Angeles through Chicago and I was working with Eddy [Palchak] and we'd have to make sure all the equipment got on that second flight. I remember one time a skate sharpener wound up in Hawaii."

Gervais said FedEx is a valuable ally.

"We use them a lot if we need something in a hurry or if [Tomas Plekanec] is in Czech during the summer and he needs some skates," said Gervais.

The Canadiens supply all the players' equipment.

"Even if a player has a deal with Bauer or CCM, we still have to pay for all the equipment," said Gervais.

Skates and sticks account for the largest portion of the equipment budget.

"Some guys change their skates every three weeks," said Gervais. "The skates today are light and comfortable. You don't have to break them in. You can wear them for the first time in the morning skate and then play with them that night. The performance is unbelievable, but they don't last. If you look at a pair of skates a guy has had for two or three weeks, you'd think he had them for two or three months. They wear out pretty fast. They're more expensive, and they don't last as long.

"It's the same with sticks," added Gervais. "When Easton came out with their composite sticks, they said they're more expensive, but they'll last for three, four, five games. Forget about it. A lot of guys have a new stick every game. When they first came out, they were five times more expensive than wood sticks. The accounting people were going bananas because of the bills. They came down and said: 'What's with the bills?' and we showed them that's how it is. You have to give the players what they want."

Gervais is also responsible for ensuring that the dressing rooms at the Bell Centre and at the practice facility in Brossard are clean. An outbreak of staph infections in NFL locker rooms in 2014 and a number of mumps cases in the NHL in the 2014–15 season led to this emphasis on clean locker rooms.

"We strip the rooms down and disinfect them on a regular basis, and we also take extra precautions whenever there's a flu bug going around."

Rewriting History

In 2005, noted Quebec film director Charles Binamé produced *The Rocket*, a movie about Canadiens legend Maurice (Rocket) Richard.

The movie depicted Richard's early struggles to establish himself as an NHL player and ended with the dramatic events surrounding his suspension and the infamous Richard Riot on March 17, 1955.

Binamé went to great pains to ensure that the film was as accurate as possible. Head writer Ken Scott worked closely with Richard before his death and also conferred with former players, Richard's wife, and the player's longtime barber.

Current NHL players were enlisted to lend authenticity to the on-ice scenes. Vinnie Lecavalier portrayed Jean Béliveau; Philippe Sauvé was cast as Boston goaltender Sugar Jim Henry; Stéphane

Quintal played Dollard St. Laurent; Ian Laperriere played Bernie Geoffrion; and Mike Ricci appeared as Elmer Lach.

For all their attempts at getting it right, the film contained one major gaffe as noted by former colleague and current NHL.com historian Dave Stubbs.

As Stubbs recalled, he discussed the movie with Lach, and they agreed that having Ricci portray the Hall of Famer was an inspired choice because, if for no other reason, both had prominent noses.

"But they got one thing wrong, and I asked Elmer if he knew what it was," said Stubbs. "He said he thought everything was good. Then, I pointed out to him that there was a scene with Elmer sitting in the dressing room the night of the Richard riot. I said: 'You weren't there, you retired the year before.'"

A FEW WORDS
OF THANKS

I owe my love of hockey to my father. I grew up in New York, and my father had played some hockey as a teenager before the basketball coach at St. Michael's High School in Brooklyn decided that his 6-foot-3 frame was better suited for basketball.

My mother was not a fan—she thought the sport was too violent, but later in life she embraced the Islanders when my father bought season tickets. She would not allow us to watch hockey on the TV in the living room, so I would join my father and my brothers in the basement rec room where we would watch the Rangers and Gillette Friday Night Fights.

I was a Rangers fan, but my allegiance changed after I read Ed Fitzgerald's book, *Champions in Sport and Spirit*. Fitzgerald, who was the editor of *Sport Magazine* and later a driving force behind the Book of the Month Club, chronicled the exploits of Catholic athletes. It was required reading for boys attending parochial schools.

There was a story about Brooklyn Dodgers first baseman Gil Hodges, who was already one of my heroes.

There was Bob Cousy, the Boston Celtics star who led the College of the Holy Cross to an NCAA championship.

And there was Maurice Richard of the Montreal Canadiens, whose scoring prowess earned him the nickname Rocket.

Richard was in the twilight of his career in 1956, but I was fascinated by Fitzgerald's portrait of this fierce competitor. I was glued to the TV each time the Canadiens played the Rangers, and I began rooting for this team from an exotic foreign land.

Twelve years later, I found myself in Richard's basement, and I watched him spool fishing line that offered anglers success if only because it carried the Rocket's name. I was in the early days of a career that has spanned more than 50 years, and there are so many people I have to thank for contributing to whatever success I've achieved.

The nuns at Our Lady of Loretto encouraged my earliest attempts at writing, and the Jesuits at Regis High School gave me the gift of logic. My high school English teacher, Pat Walsh, opened his home to me and steered me into journalism and to Canada.

I'm grateful to Harold Atkins for taking a chance on me and giving me my first job at the *Montreal Star* where I was mentored by Ian McDonald, Red Fisher, and Elmer Ferguson, who was at the Windsor Hotel in Montreal to cover the birth of the NHL in 1917. Red gave me my first chance to write about the Canadiens and provided me with guidance, support, and, most importantly, friendship through the years.

I've had the privilege of working alongside some of the greatest names in Canadian sports journalism—Red Fisher, Michael Farber, Jim Coleman, Scott Young, Dink Carroll, Milt Dunnell, Jim Taylor, James Lawton, and Bob McDevitt, who taught me how to write for radio and TV.

I'm grateful to the editors who hired me and gave me a chance to see more of my adopted homeland: Mel Morris at the *Toronto Star* and the *Montreal Gazette*; Clark Davey at the *Globe and Mail*, the *Vancouver Sun*, and my final stint at the *Montreal Gazette*; Ian Urquhart, Lou Clancy, and Mary Deanne Shears at the *Toronto Star* and George (the Baron) Gross at the *Toronto Sun*.

In researching this book, I started with my memories and matched them against the stories—many of them my own—in the files of the defunct *Montreal Star* and the *Montreal Gazette*.

The research proved that memories may be great, but they are not always accurate. I am grateful for the source material produced by colleagues Red Fisher, Michael Farber, Stu Cowan, Jack Todd, Herb Zurkowsky, Dave Stubbs, and Bob Morrissey.

Over the years, I've conducted hundreds of interviews with Canadiens players and executives, but I offer special thanks to Réjean Houle, who offered his perspective on the team and also facilitated interviews with Serge Savard, Guy Lafeur, Chris Nilan, Yvan Cournoyer, and Peter Mahovlich.

Thanks also to Donald Beauchamp, Dominick Saillant, François Marchand, Carl Lavigne, and Sylvie Lambert of the Canadiens public relations staff for their help through the years.

Finally, I would like to thank Bill, Adam, Jesse, and the folks at Triumph Books for another opportunity to work with them.

Any opinions expressed in this book are my own, and I also take responsibility for any mistakes.